T0352088

An Essay on the Early History
of the Law Merchant

An Essay on the Early History of the Law Merchant

being the Yorke Prize Essay for the year 1903

by

W. MITCHELL, B.A.

St Catharine's College,
Assistant Master at the Perse School, Cambridge

Cambridge :
at the University Press
1904

CAMBRIDGE UNIVERSITY PRESS
Cambridge, New York, Melbourne, Madrid, Cape Town,
Singapore, São Paulo, Delhi, Tokyo, Mexico City

Cambridge University Press
The Edinburgh Building, Cambridge CB2 8RU, UK

Published in the United States of America by
Cambridge University Press, New York

www.cambridge.org
Information on this title: www.cambridge.org/9780521233231

© Cambridge University Press 1904

First published 1904
First paperback edition 2011

A catalogue record for this publication is available from the British Library

ISBN 978-0-521-23323-1 Paperback

PREFACE.

THIS Essay does not in any way claim to be a Treatise on the subject. Lack of leisure has compelled me to omit many important topics and to deal ·all too briefly with others. My debt to previous writers—to Bensa, Huvelin, Schaube, Pollock and Maitland, and above all to Goldschmidt —is evident on every page; as far as time and opportunities allowed I have gone to the original authorities. While the Essay was in the Press, I learnt that there were numerous fair rolls preserved in the Record Office and upon these I am at work. To Sir F. Pollock for kind suggestions I wish to express my thanks.

CONTENTS

CHAPTER   PAGE

I.   GENERAL CHARACTERISTICS   .   .   . 1

II.   THE RISE OF THE LAW MERCHANT   . . 22

III.   THE COURTS OF THE LAW MERCHANT . . 39

IV.   PERSONS   79

V.   SALES AND CONTRACTS 93

CONCLUSION 156

APPENDIX I 162

APPENDIX II   164

APPENDIX III   165

APPENDIX IV   167

APPENDIX V   168

AUTHORITIES   169

INDEX   173

CORRIGENDA

P. 34, footnote. *Read* Bruschettini
P. 84, line 8. *Omit* for

CHAPTER I.

GENERAL CHARACTERISTICS.

THE Law Merchant has been aptly called "the private international law of the Middle Ages." It was regarded as a kind of jus gentium known to all the merchants throughout Christendom and the later writers who treated the subject laid stress upon its international character[1]. "The Law Merchant," wrote Sir John Davies in the 17th century, "as it is part of the law of nature and nations is one and the same in all the countries in the world; there is not one law in England, another in France, another in Germany, but the same rules of reason and the like proceedings are observed in every nation." This statement is too sweeping. Strictly construed it was not correct for the law as it existed in the 17th

[1] Malynes, *Lex Mercatoria*, 3. "The said customary law of merchants hath a peculiar prerogative above all other customs, for that the same is observed in all places."

Davies, *The Question concerning Impositions*, 10. "That commonwealth of merchants hath always had a peculiar and proper law to rule and govern it; this law is called the Law Merchant whereof the law of all nations do take special knowledge."

century, and it was still less correct for the Law
Merchant in the earlier stages of its evolution.
There was during the early middle ages no strictly
uniform system of mercantile law administered
throughout the whole of Western Europe either
in town or seaport or fair. The Great Fairs of
Champagne had their own style, usage and customs
which were at times altered in important points by
royal ordinance. The Merchants of Antwerp refused[1]
to submit to the law of London, and in the numerous
"lettres de foires" that have recently been discovered
at Ypres[2] the alien creditor has always to promise
not to recover his debt by any other law than the
law of Ypres. In Italy the special codes of commerce
that almost every great city possessed, show greater
or smaller discrepancies in almost every section, and
as a natural result, in several cities[3], the commercial

[1] *Monumenta Gildhallae*, vol. II. part i. 63. "Et cil de
Anwers ne passeront le pount de Loundres, si il ne voillent estre
desmenez par la ley de Loundres."

[2] Des Marez, *La Lettre de foire à Ypres*, p. 97 and
document 27. "Et li avant di Jehans de Flaringhes, borgois de
St Quentin, a encovent et promis par foit ke il ceste dette ne
requerra a nule loi fors a la loi de la ville d'Ypre."

[3] Statutes of Como, *Monumenta Historiae Patriae*, vol. XVI.
col. 28, cap. xxxi. A.D. 1281. "Quod ipsi consules possint cognoscere de omnibus quaestionibus negociatorum forensium et de
negociacionibus...quamcunque quantitatem ascendant et hoc tam
in cognoscendo quam in diffiniendo et execucioni mandando‖
eisdem mercatoribus talem faciant et facere possint racionem et
non aliter, qualiter fieret mercatoribus Cumanis‖in terra illius
mercatoris tunc querentis sub eisdem consulibus."

A.D. 1352. Spalati St. Nova, cap. xxvii. p. 246 (in *Monumenta Historico-Juridica Slavorum Meridionalium*). "Ordinatum
est quod amodo illud jus et justicia quod et que fiet civibus...

judges were ordered to give aliens no better law than their own citizens would have in the alien state.

Sometimes the variations in the Law were of far-reaching importance, and perhaps no better example can be given than the rules regulating the effect of Earnest money. Here, if anywhere, a definite and universal rule might be expected, for otherwise no merchant could be sure of his bargain. In the 13th century, however, the effect of the Earnest had not been finally settled. As a general rule it may be said that the payment of a God's penny was effectual to bind a mercantile bargain, and Fleta expressly declares that such was the law amongst merchants. Edward I., for instance, gave the Earnest a binding force, as a favour to the foreign merchants. " Every contract," ran a clause in the Carta Mercatoria, "between the said merchants and any persons whencesoever they may come, touching any kind of merchandise, shall be firm and stable, so that neither of the said merchants shall be able to retract or resile from the said contract when once the God's penny shall have been given and received[1]." At Avignon[1] the same rule prevailed; but there were exceptions. The Preston custumal[2] allowed the

Spalati in quacunque curia et foro cujuscunque civitatis...illud simile jus et justicia per similem modum et formam fiat in curia et foro civitatis illis hominibus."

1429. St. Merc. Brixiae, cap. 43. "Etiam possunt [consules mercatorum] forensibus tale jus reddere quale et quem ad modum in eorum terris redditur nostratibus."

[1] Maitland, *Select Pleas in Manorial Courts*, 133.

[2] Custumal of Preston, Article 12. Bateson, *Eng. Hist. Review* (1900), p. 497. "Item si Burgensis aliquid forum vel

seller to break the contract by repaying double the
Earnest, and the buyer by forfeiting five shillings.
In Italy most of the commercial statutes[1] declare
that if once an Earnest is accepted the contract is
binding, but Varese[2] again offers an exception to the
general rule, while in Sicily[3] it was the custom among
merchants to consider the Earnest merely as a

aliquem mercem emerit et hernas dederit et ille qui vendiderit de
foro suo penitebit duplicabit hernas ementis. Si autem emens
forum suum palpabit vel habebit forum vel quinque solidos de
vendente."

[1] Circa 1200. St. Antiqua Mercatorum Placentiae, cap. 65,
p. 20. "Et si quis de nusii (=mercantiae) jurisdictione mercatum fecerit...et...denarium dei dederit vel dari fecerit, illud
mercatum inter partes ratum haberi faciam."

1214, confirmed in 1265. St. Legis civitatis et insulae Curzulae
(in *M.H.S.M.*), cap. xxxv. p. 15. "Si quis mercatur emendo
aliquid ab aliquo dederit unum denarium parvum pro arris,
mercator sit firmum et venditor teneatur dare et emptor recipere
merces: ab uno denario supra si aliquis dederit arràs, pro quo
remanebit mercatum, ille teneatur solvere alteri parti arras in
duplum." Cf. p. 36, cap. 38.

1302. Florence. St. Calimalae, Lb. iii. cap. i. "Quo denario
dato mercatum stabile sit et firmum."

1312. Spalati vetus statutum, Lb. iii. cap. 96, p. 109 (in
M.H.S.M.). "Si...arre date fuerint...dictum mercatum sit firmum
et ratum...quia nihil tam contingit fidei humane congruum quam
ea que juste per pactum inter aliquos intervenerunt observari."

14th century. St. Scardonae (in *M.H.S.M.*), cap. x. p. 122.
"Si aliquas arras dederit, illud mercatum nec emptor nec venditor
valeat relinquere."

[2] 1347. Lattes, *Diritto Commerciale*, p. 132, note 14.
"Quando le merci fossero state spalmate o benedicte, chi mancava
al contratto dovesse risarcire ogni danno, invece se si fosse
soltanto data la caparra, chi l' aveva dato dovesse perderla, chi l'
aveva ricevuta, restituire il doppio." Quoted from St. de Varisio.

[3] Brunneck, *Siciliens Mittelalterliche Stadtrechte*, p. 186,
note 1.

penalty for breach of contract until a law of Frederick II. forbade the custom. There are signs of the same uncertainty in Germany. At Hildesheim[1], in the middle of the 13th century, the Earnest did not make the contract binding, while according to the custumal of 1300 it did.

Maritime Law again, which showed great uniformity in later times, was far from uniform during the Middle Ages. Numerous local laws and customs existed which were gradually supplanted in the North by the Laws of Oleron and Wisby, and in the South by the Laws of Barcelona. It was a slow process, however, for as late as the 17th century the code of Amalfi[2] was recognised in Southern Italy, while legislation in England, Holland and France soon began to create fresh divergences.

But it is perhaps in the fairs, where special courts existed for administering the Law Merchant, that strict uniformity might most naturally be expected; for here the international element was unusually strong. Foreigners are judged in the Fair Court of St Ives[3]; Spanish, Italian, French and

[1] 1249. Stadtrecht of Hildesheim, cap. 23. (In *Hildesheim Urkundenbuch*, vol. I. no. 209.) "Si quis aliquid emerit et aliquam summam super eo dederit quod dicitur 'oringe,' si idem vult retractet ipse amittet summam quam dederit; si vero venditor retractare voluerit, ipse summam quam accepit restituet et postea duplo restituet ipsam summam que dicitur 'oringe.'"

Circa 1300. Stadtrecht, cap. 152, no. 548, p. 294. "Koft me enne kop und gift me dar enne goddespenning up, de kop scal stede sin."

[2] v. Wagner, *Seerecht*, p. 37, note 7.

[3] v. cases in court of St Ives. Maitland, *Select Pleas*, pp. 152, 155.

German merchants are among the contracting parties in the bonds of the Fair of Ypres[1], while to the great Fairs of Champagne merchants streamed from every part of Europe. But even in fairs there is evidence to show that the Law is not everywhere identical. When Edward I. declared in the Carta Mercatoria that all plaints of foreigners should be decided according to the Law Merchant, he added that if any dispute should arise as to their contracts with any persons, proof and inquiry should be made according to the usages and customs of the fairs and market towns where the contract had been made[2]. Evidently the usages and customs of fairs differed. Equally significant is the statute of Westminster of 1275. " It is ordained," ran one of its clauses, " that in any city, borough town, fair or market, a foreign person who is of this realm shall not be distrained for any debt for which he is not debtor or pledge." This changed the law as observed in English towns and fairs, and created a difference between the usage in England and in other countries. In Northern Italy a long series[3] of treaties—many of later date

[1] Des Marez, *La Lettre de foire à Ypres*. See documents, nos. 68, 73, 74, 77, 81, 84.

[2] *Monumenta Gildhallae*, II. i. p. 206. " Et si forsan super contractu hujusmodi contentio oriatur, fiat inde probatio vel inquisitio secundum usus et consuetudines feriarum et villarum mercatoriarum ubi dictum contractum fieri contigerit et iniri."

[3] See the many treaties printed in *I trattati commerciali della Repubblica Fiorentina* by Arias. The treaty of 1279 included all Venice, Genoa, and all the cities of Tuscany, Lombardy and Romagna. Fairs are not specially mentioned, but the terms of the treaty are so general as to include them. This treaty provided that " nullus dictarum civitatum possit vel debeat pro

than Edward's legislation—was slowly and fitfully securing for the Italians this same protection against distraint for the debts of a fellow-citizen. The law, however, for long remained unchanged and in the case of absence or repudiation of a treaty, the Italian had no protection.

In England it seems that at one time the procedure adopted in fairs and towns against absent defendants varied so much that a 14th century treatise on the " Lex Mercatoria[1] " declared that no one could know or ascertain the procedure of the Law Merchant on this point. Uniformity in this particular was, however, established in the end, and probably with the aid of the royal authority[2].

Still, in spite of minor differences, the international character of the Law Merchant as administered in the fair courts cannot be denied. " The customs of different places may have varied slightly, but the law in its broad lines was necessarily of that international character which has always been its chief characteristic." Nor is this true only of the law administered in fairs. The same general

alio detineri vel capi vel etiam inquietari in persona vel rebus, sed cui datum fuerit illi solum requiratur vel illi qui de jure teneretur." Arias, p. 402.

[1] Bickley, *The Little Red Book of Bristol*, p. 62. "Et ita diversimode in diversis partibus quod nullus omnino processum legis mercatorie in ea parte scire nec cognoscere poterit."

[2] Bickley, *The Little Red Book of Bristol*, p. 62. The new uniform regulations which are evidently intended to apply to the whole kingdom are introduced by " propter hoc ordinatum est." Uniformity was secured not by custom, but by regulation from above.

agreement upon the main rules and principles, with the same divergences upon less important points, characterize all the commercial codes and customs of Europe. The Law Merchant, in fact, was vague and indefinite; in many of its courts the law was regarded as a purely customary law to be declared, in case of doubt, by the merchants of the courts themselves, and even where its rules had been codified there were in reserve unwritten rules founded on custom which the commercial judges were ordered to observe[1]. But in spite of its vagueness the Law

[1] A.D. 1281. St. of Como in *Monumenta Historiae Patriae,* vol. XVI. column 15. "Eadem [placita] definiam...secundum statuta pertinentia ad officium mercatorum, et deficientibus ipsis statutis secundum alia statuta consulum Cumarum justiciae et civitatis Cumarum, deficientibus ipsis secundum usus et bonos mores civitatis ejusdem approbatos, et his deficientibus secundum leges et jura."

1305. Pisa. *Breve Curiae Mercatorum,* c. 9. (Bonaini, vol. III. p. 12.) "Et si qua reclamatio coram me...de minori quantitate solidorum XL denariorum fuerit facta ipsam diffiniam... secundum usum pisanae civitatis et consuetudinem mercatorum."

1305. *Eodem,* c. 6, p. 10. "Si constitutum inde non est in causa hujus, secundum bonum usum civitatis Pisanae et mercatantie."

1305. *Eodem,* c. 81, p. 59. "Et juro quod observabo et tenebo omnes et singulas bonas consuetudines et bonos usus quae et qui fieri consueverunt in suprascripta curia in terminando lites et causas."

1250. St. Bologna of 1250, Lb. iv. cap. 19 a. "Quod jus fori et mercati reddatur secundum consuetudinem fori sive mercati."

1237. Commercial Treaty between Florence and Sien (Arias, *op. cit.* 373). "Teneantur arbitri...omnes lites...diffinire...secundum jura et bonum usum mercantiae utriusque terrae."

1400. St. Merc. Mantuae, c. 2. "Omnes lamentationes et querimonias mihi factas a meis negociatoribus diffiniam secundum

Merchant existed. In every commercial country in Europe there were rules and legal doctrines for merchants and mercantile transactions that were regarded alike by merchants and by jurists as distinct from the common law of the land.

These rules and doctrines, which were distinct, it must be repeated, from the common law, were the Law Merchant. Each country, it may almost be said each town, had its own variety of Law Merchant, yet all were but varieties of the same species. Everywhere the leading principles and the most important rules were the same, or tended to become the same. It is the growth and development of these common rules and underlying principles that constitute the history of the Law Merchant. No doubt, in each country the Law Merchant to a certain

rationem et bonam consuetudinem negociacionis et secundum statutum mercadandiae."

1161. Prologue to *Constitutum usus* of Pisa (Bonaini, vol. II. and Pertile, I. p. 395, note 35). "Pisana itaque civitas propter conversationem diversarum gentium per diversas mundi partes, suas consuetudines non scriptas habere meruit, super quas annuatim judices posuit, quos previsores appellavit, ut ex equitate pro salute justitiae, et honore et salvamento civitatis, tam civibus quam advenis et peregrinis et omnibus universaliter in consuetudinibus praeviderent....Unde Pisani...consuetudines suas quas propter conversationem quam cum diversis gentibus habuerunt, et huc usque in memoriam retinuerunt, in scriptis statuerunt redigendas, pro cognitione omnium ea scire volentium."

It is to be noted that of the five "previsores" only one was to be a jurisperitus, and that a copy of the "constitutum usus" was always to be in the "curia maris" for any one belonging to the Sea Gild (aliquis de ordine maris) to consult. See Schaube, *Das Consulat des Meeres in Pisa*, pp. 127 and 129.

extent traced out its own curve of progress. The English Law Merchant has its history, no less than the Italian. But neither alone is the history of the Law Merchant. This essay has for its object to trace the development of the common essential elements that are found in the early Law Merchant of every country. The scope of the subject is not narrow and I can only attempt briefly to touch upon what seem the most important points.

The Law Merchant, then, was a body of rules and principles relating to merchants and mercantile transactions, distinct from the ordinary law of the land. Possessed of a certain uniformity in its essential features, it yet differed on minor points from place to place. The question at once arises, in what did this uniformity of character consist? To this question only a close investigation can give a complete answer, but the essential features of the Law Merchant and the broad general principles that permanently influenced its development, are clearly marked and can be stated at the outset.

In the first place, the Law Merchant was in the main customary law. "The grandeur and significance of the medieval merchant," says Goldschmidt, "is that he creates his own laws out of his own needs and his own views." Early in the 11th century, the German merchants were already asserting the force of their own customs against the common law. "Merchants assert," said Notker[1],

---

[1] Keutgen, *Urkunden*, no. 74, p. 44. "Also choufliute stritent, tas der chouf sule wesen state, der ze jarmercate getan wurdet, er si reht alde unreht, wanda iz iro gewoneheite ist."

"that sales made in fairs, whether made with proper legal forms or not, should be binding, since it is their custom." A few years later the merchants of Tiel[1] are described as deciding cases not according to the law, but as they wished. In Italy the commercial judges based their decisions upon custom and upon mercantile statutes[2] framed for the most part by the Merchant Gild, though confirmed by the State. The Bristol Treatise[3] on the Lex Mercatoria shows clearly that in England the force of custom was recognised. Everywhere, in commercial transactions, custom held sway, and even where the State legislated it had often merely to confirm or slightly modify the rules that had long before been established by custom.

The earliest English statute on Insurance, of the year 1601, declares that it "hathe been tyme out of mynde an usage among merchants," while similarly

---

[1] Keutgen, A.D. 1018, *Urkunden*, no. 75. "Judicia non secundum legem sed secundum voluntatem decernentes." Cf. Freiburg Stadtrecht of 1120 (Keutgen, no. 133, c. 5, p. 118). "Disceptatio...pro consuetudinario et legitimo jure omnium mercatorum, praecipue autem Coloniensium examinabitur judicio."

[2] v. quotations, pp. 8, 9.

[3] In *Little Red Book of Bristol*, vol. I. c. 4, p. 60. "Sed apponitur adhuc le affidavit propter antiquam consuetudinem."

c. 21, p. 83. "Ut ipsi...fieri facerent quod de jure et secundum legem et consuetudinem mercatoriam fuerit faciendum."

For maritime law cf. *Black Book of Admiralty*, p. 3. The Admiral is to appoint as deputies "Some of the most loyal, wise and discreete persons in the law maratime and ancient customs of the sea."

Black Book of Admiralty, vol. I. p. 168. Additions to *Inquisition of Queensborough*, cap. 71. "Est de faire sommaire et plain proces selon loy marine et ancienne coustume de la mer." Cf. p. 409.

on the Continent the early statutes dealing with insurance only legislated upon minor points, leaving the main points to be decided by custom[1]. "In all great matters relating to commerce the legislators have copied, not dictated."

This customary nature of the Law Merchant was by far the most decisive factor in its development: it made the law eminently a practical law adapted to the requirements of commerce; and as trade expanded and new forms of commercial activity arose —negotiable paper, insurance, etc.—custom everywhere fashioned and framed the broad general principles of the new law. Custom is alike the ruling principle and the originating force of the Law Merchant.

The summary nature of its jurisdiction is a second feature that always characterised the Lex Mercatoria. Its justice was prompt, its procedure summary, and often the time within which disputes must be finally settled was narrowly limited[2]. To

---

[1] Goldschmidt, *Handbuch des Handelsrecht*, pp. 374—5, 378—9.

[2] 12th cent. Rouen. *Établissements*, c. 26. "Si quis requisierit curiam suam de debitis, conceditur ei, et faciat rectum clamius in *duabus octonis.*"

The customs of Rouen were received in many French cities. See Gory's edition.

1302. Florence. St. Calimalae, Lb. ii. c. 2. "Et teneantur consules finire et terminare hujusmodi quaestiones...intra *XL.* dies."

12th cent. Pisa. *Constitutum usus*, c. 11. "Et post quam liquet, infra *octo* dies eam diffiniat."

1305. Pisa. *Breve Maris*, c. 19. "Omnes causas infra *tertium* diem ex quo mihi liquebit...diffiniam, nisi justa causa remanserit."

prevent lengthy processes it is not rare to find appeals forbidden[1]. Speedy justice, in fact, was necessary for merchants, and while the Canon Law[2] and the usage of the Papal Chancery may have furthered the development of this summary procedure in the Law Merchant, there can be no doubt that it was mainly due to the necessity experienced by the merchants themselves[3] of a speedy settlement of their disputes. This characteristic feature of the Law Merchant seems especially to have struck the 14th century author of the Bristol Treatise. " The Lex Mercati," he remarks, "differs from the common

1400. St. Merc. Mantuae, c. 2. "Omnes lamentationes et querimonias...occasione mercadandiae diffiniam et determinabo infra *unum mensem.*"

1286. St. of Como. Cases "inter mercatores occasione mercationum" to be decided "infra xv dies utiles," between other persons "infra duos menses."

[1] 1286. *Breve Pisani communis*, Lb. i. c. 61 (Bonaini, I. p. 155). "Omnes sententiae quae feruntur a consulibus ordinis maris de naulo et marinatico et de avere guasto, a libris centum infra valeant...a quibus sententiis non possit appellari."

See numerous references in Lattes, *Diritto Commerciale*, p. 279, note 59.

[2] 1306. The Decretal "Clementina Saepe" of Clement VI. dealt with the summary procedure, and there is a striking analogy in substance and form between the language of the Italian Statutes and the Decretal. See Lattes, *Studii di diritto statuario*, p. 51.

[3] Goldschmidt quotes (p. 174) from St. Merc. of Verona (p. 114).

1406. " More mercationis expedite et breviter procedatur, quia bene scitis quod mercatorum conditio longitudines non requirat." Cf. Bonaini, III. 207 note.

1384. "Si mercatorum negotia ad litigatorum tergiversationes et judicales observantias reducantur, peribit de societate mortalium mercatura."

law of the realm in three ways; in the first place[1]
'quod celerius deliberat se ipsam.' 'The plees,' says
the Domesday Book of Ipswich[2], 'betwixe straunge
folk that men clepeth pypoudrous shouldene ben
pleted from day to day if the pleyntiff or the de-
fendaunt preye of suche aiourning. The plees in
time of fair betwixe straunge and passant shouldene
beene pleted from hour to hour as well in the fore-
noon as afternoon......and the plees yoven to the
law maryne, that is to wit for straunge maryners
passant and for hem that abyden not but her tyde,
should be pleted from tide to tide.'" The desire for
despatch expressed itself in many ways but everywhere the principle is evident. In Italy[3] almost all
the commercial statutes of the various cities instructed

[1] *Lex Mercatoria*, c. 2.

[2] *Black Book of Admiralty*, vol. II. pp. 22, 23.

[3] St. of Brescia (1313), Lb. iii. c. 59 (*Monumenta Historiae
Patriae*, vol. XVI. column 1737). The "consules mercatorum"
in cases "de mercatis et rebus mobilibus pertinentibus ad
mercathendiam" are to proceed "summarie sine porrectione
libelli et litis contestione et sine strepitu juditiorum, ita quod
processus...valeat et teneat ac si rigor juris esset solemniter et
integre observatus."

A.D. 1403—7. *Leges Genuenses* (edited by Poggi in *M.H.P.*,
column 537).

1403—7. "Causae quae inter mercatores Januenses orientur
causa mercandi...magistratus teneatur...diffinire summarie et de
plano sine strepitu et figura judicii."

1302. Florence. St. Calimalae, Lb. ii. c. 2. "Sine contestione
litis et qualibet juris solemnitate strepituque judicii." (Also in
Italian version of 1332.)

See numerous references in Lattes, *Diritto Commerciale*, p. 267,
note 2.

the judges to use a summary procedure. At Pisa[1] it was in maritime law at first confined to a limited number of cases, but in the later statutes of the city the procedure gradually gained ground. At Marseilles[2], where the existence of commercial judges dates from the 12th century, it was their duty to decide cases and disputes between merchants "summarily, without regard to the subtleties of the law." The German Hanse, the English and French Admiralty all administered summary justice[3]. For the passing stranger or the foreign merchant *en route*, a specially prompt justice was generally the

---

[1] 1248. "Quaestio marinariatici et nauli, et de mercibus amissis seu deterioratis in navi...summatim...dirimatur" (*Constitutum usus*, c. 11).

1259. "De mercedibus hominum et vecturis animalium idem observatur."

1281. "Potestas...de litibus...contra magistros lignaminum et murorum et contra alios opifices pro eorum artificio, debeat summatim...cognoscere et eas finire infra 8 dies."

1286. "Si inter creditores de bonis obligatis aut ypoteca bonorum quaestio fuerit, summatim de plano, etc."

v. Pertile, vol. VI. ii. p. 116, note 10. Schaube (*Das Consulat des Meeres in Pisa*) deals fully with this development of summary procedure in Pisa, pp. 135—6.

[2] See Morel, *Les Juridictions Commerciales au Moyen Age*, pp. 135—7.

[3] *Black Book of Admiralty*, p. 409. It was the duty of the deputy of the English High Admiral "to make summary and hasty process from tide to tide according to the ancient law marine and ancient customs of the sea without observing the solemnity of the law." For French admiralty see ordonnance of 1373 (in *Black Book of Admiralty*, p. 480), "Sera tenue la juridiction du dit admiral...de jour en jour et d'heure en autre."

rule¹; it was felt that the usual procedure, prompt as it was, did not meet their case.

Thirdly, the Law Merchant was characterized by the spirit of equity. In the 18th century an English judge² spoke of the Lex Mercatoria as "a system of equity founded on rules of equity and governed in all its parts by plain justice and good faith." "In the plaints (causis) of merchants," declare the Gild Statutes of Bergamo for 1457, "equity is especially to be considered and the cases are to be decided 'ex aequo et bono'; it is not meet to dispute on the subtleties of the Law." At Aquila³ the consuls (1396) were to inquire into "the pure and simple truth, as the usage and equity of merchants demanded, and

¹ Grimm, *Rechtsalterthümer*, I. 556. "Keme ein fremder man und begehrte ein notgericht, dem soll man unverzogenliche gehorsam sein."

c. 1200. St. Antiqua Merc. Placentiae, c. 633. "Consules mercadandie debeant facere cuilibet foresterio conquerenti de aliquo civitatis et districtus summariam et brevissimam rationem."

1214. St. Cuzulae (in *M.H.S.M.*, p. 35), cap. 35. "Si viatores...forenses contra homines insulae placitare voluerint de aliqua ratione eodem die contracta, homo insulae teneatur sibi statim sine aliquo termino respondere; et si ille forensis traheret hic moram, respondeat sibi usque ad duos dies et sicut homo insulae tenetur forensibus respondere." (Confirmed 1265, p. 15, c. 32.)

1312. St. vetus Spalati (in *M.H.S.M.*), c. 5, p. 9. "Quaestiones forensium mercatorum possint etiam quocunque tempore agitari tam in dictis festivitatibus et diebus feriatis quam et non feriatis......ut possint sine mora et dilatione aliqua expediri."

Cf. Domesday of Ipswich, and Silberschmidt, *Die Entstehung des deutschen Handelsgerichts*, p. 31.

² Buller, J., in Master *v.* Miller (4 T.R., 320).

³ 1395. Muratori, *Antiq. Ital.*, VI. 788, quoted by Pertile, VII. p. 114, note 9.

as it was wont to be done in mercantile actions and affairs," and the consuls of Bologna (1279) gave judgment "secundum quod aequum crediderint[1]." In Venice by a decree of the Council (1287) the consuls of the merchants were to swear to decide disputes according to custom, and if custom failed them, "secundum bonam conscientiam[2]." At Marseilles[3] the same spirit prevailed and the judges were to decide suits between merchants "sans s'atteindre aux subtilités des lois et des ordonnances[3]." England, however, lagged behind. It was mainly an agricultural, not a commercial country, and its commercial jurisprudence developed slowly. The records of the Fair Court of St Ives[4] show that formalism and technicalities still held their ground. Verbal

[1] 1279. Stat. Mercat. Florent. Bon., quoted by Pertile, vi. i. p. 113, note 8.

[2] 1287. Quoted by Lattes, *Il Diritto Commerciale*, p. 73, note 1.

1302. St. Calimalae, Lb. ii. c. 2. "Item quod in quaestionibus xxv. librarum vel infra consules possint procedere in cognoscendo et sententiendo ad eorum arbitrium et voluntatem."

1305. Pisa. St. Mercatorum, c. 81 (Bonaini, iii. 59). "Possimus nos consules...cognoscere diffinire et arbitrari praecipere quidquid nobis...*videbitur aequum* de omnibus et singulis erroribus et dolis et fraudibus."

1384. Letter from Signoria of Florence to commune of Pisa (Bonaini, iii. 207). "Hanc autem litem audivimus non aequitate mercatoria discuti, sed ad judiciorum calumnias coartari......sed *in aequitate mercatoria* visa simplici veritate sine morae dispendio dirimatur."

[3] Edict of 1565. "Ont été créés et institués *de toute ancienneté* par le conseil de la ville deux juges des marchands pour juger et décider......Sans s'atteindre *aux subtilités des lois* et des ordonnances." Quoted by Morel, *op. cit.*, p. 136.

[4] Maitland, *Select Pleas in Manorial Courts*, 136.

accuracy was required of the defendant and it was
possible for a debtor to defraud his creditor and
prevent attachment of his goods by going through
the farce of a mock sale. An equitable procedure,
however, was in English towns slowly supplanting
the old system. The Leicester Charter[1] of 1277
may be taken as an example. " Whereas," declares
the preamble, "the delays of the Portmanmoot of
Leicester have been too long and some usages have
injured those who had to sue their right, Sir Edmund,
Lord of the aforesaid town,......by his council and by
the assent of the Mayor and the Jurates and the
whole community of the same town, has ordered and
provided the amendments underwritten. In the
first place because it happened that when a man
impleaded another for debts or trespass, half a year
or a whole year often passed before he could bring
his adversary to answer, partly by reason of the
feeble distress of the bailiffs, and partly because men
hid their goods in rooms or elsewhere, so that no one
could distrain them......let order to distrain be issued
to make him attend the Third Court by the great
distress by whatsoever may be found of his within
his house or without, so that if he causes his goods to
be hidden or shut up in a room or elsewhere, the
bailiff by view of the neighbours may enter everywhere to distrain him till justice be done......And
whereas it was customary heretofore when the
parties ought to plead and the plaintiff had said his
plaint, if the defendant directly the plea had left
the plaintiff's mouth did not say 'Thwerthutnay' he

---

[1] Bateson, *Records of Leicester*, I. 150.

was held to be non-defendant, and that was called
Swarless, and he was not allowed to plead nor to ask
council nor have any man who knew the usages to
speak for him, whereby many from not knowing the
usages lost their suits: for this it is now provided,
that when the parties appear and ought to plead,
let the plaintiff fully state his case, without challenge
or hindrance, by himself, if he knows how, or if not
by another who is avowed, so that the suit shall not
be abated by non-specification of time or by any
other circumstances challenged. But if the defendant demands declaration of time or other thing
necessary to the plaint that he may be better certain
of answering, let the declaration be made at the same
time without challenge......And if he trow that his
first answer does not suffice, let him say something
else to which he is willing to hold absolutely and upon
which he will take judgment......And whereas it was
heretofore the custom that the defendant could not
answer any other thing to the plaintiff's plea except
to admit everything or to say fully a 'thwart-nay,'
and when he had said the nay, he had to be at his
law himself the sixth hand (*i.e.*, to find five com-
purgators), then the plaintiff or a man for him
would choose folk that would not go with him for
favour of the other party or for hatred of him, and if
he could not make his law with the folk named, he
would be attainted of the whole plea, whether it
were true or false. Therefore it is provided, first
that in plea of debt if the defendant denies it and
the demandant has proved his debt by writing, tally
or by word of mouth, let him be received to make

2—2

the proof, so that if he had nothing but tally or word of mouth, let him swear first and then his witness whom he brings be examined of the hearing and of the sight, if they were at the taking of the debt or the making of the tally or if they were at the place where the debt or the tally was granted from, and according to what they prove let him recover or lose his debt." Equally reasonable are the customs of Bristol[1] in "pleas of debts, contracts and covenants," during the 14th century, while in the 15th century the Admiralty expressly acknowledges the principle of equity. It was the duty of the deputy of the High Admiral[2] "to make summary and hasty process from tide to tide according to the ancient law marine and ancient customs of the sea without observing the solemnity of the law and without mixing the law civil with the law maritime, there where it may be equitable, knowing the rights of the parties." Plain justice and good faith, disregard of technicalities and regard for "the sole truth of the matter," characterize alike in England, France, and Italy, the development of the Law Merchant.

But perhaps the most striking feature of the Law Merchant is its strongly marked international character. The main lines of development were everywhere the same, and by it foreigners were generally judged. Its rules and regulations have their origin in many lands. Pisan Laws[3] passed into

---

[1] Bickley, *Little Red Book of Bristol*, p. 40. Consuetudines, c. 31.

[2] *Black Book of Admiralty*, I. 409.

[3] Wagner, *Seerecht*, p. 39, note 11.

the sea code of Marseilles.   Oleron and Lubeck gave laws to the North of Europe, Barcelona to the South ; while from Italy came the legal principle of insurance and bills of exchange.

The international nature of the sources from which it drew its rules and of the persons over whom it exercised jurisdiction, combined with the universality of its guiding principles, fairly entitle the Law Merchant to be called " the private international law of the Middle Ages[1]."

[1] Maitland, *Select Pleas in Manorial Courts*, 133.

CHAPTER II.

THE RISE OF THE LAW MERCHANT.

THE origin of the Law Merchant, that is, of a special law for merchants and their business transactions, is closely connected with the history of commerce, fairs and markets during the troubled centuries that followed the fall of the Western Empire. Slowly during this period market and fair became an administrative and judicial unit distinct from the rest of the land, and this development is of great importance in the history of commercial law.

In the Merovingian Empire the whole land, market, fair and open country, was under the same administration. The series of charters[1] (629—759) relating to the fair of St Denis shows that the fair depended for justice and order upon the ordinary royal officials, the count and hundredman who drew no legal distinction between peasant and merchant or market and the open country. To the merchant the Merovingian Empire offered no special protection. From the Carlovingian rulers, however, merchants and commerce received more consideration.

[1] Huvelin, *Droit des Marchés*, 146—7.

Grants and confirmations of markets and fairs grew more numerous, and the crown began to place the merchants under its special protection. " You have written to us about your merchants," says Charlemagne in a letter to Offa, King of Mercia; "we would have them enjoy our protection and defence within our realm according to the ancient custom in commerce, and if in any place they are distressed by unjust oppression, let them appeal to us and we will order justice to be done. Show the same favour to our merchants." The royal protection was even granted to individual merchants, who had however generally to pay for the privilege. Jurisdiction still remained in the hands of the royal officials, but under the later Carlovingian monarchs a decisive change took place and jurisdiction over markets and fairs began to be granted to the local lords. Concessions of immunity, especially to churches and monasteries, grew common, and created a kind of preserve into which the judicial officers of the crown had no right to enter[1]. Even more important is the fact that the charters, granting to nobles or ecclesiastical foundations rights of market or fair, now contain, as a general rule, the concession of the ban, which carried with it the right of jurisdiction— " Cum omni judiciaria potestate, hoc est bannum[2]." But it was in Germany, especially during the 10th and 11th centuries, that fairs and markets were founded in greatest number and the charters are most instructive. In the first place they regularly

[1] Huvelin, *Droit des Marchés*, 160.

[2] *op. cit.* 171, vide 168—172.

grant in the plainest terms to the local lord jurisdiction over the market and freedom from the judicial
interference of the royal official. " We ordain," says
the market charter[1] of Meppen for the year 946,
"that no public judge shall exercise any judicial
power in the aforesaid place save the lawful advocate
of the aforesaid abbot." Similarly the charter of
Stade fair (1038) granted to the Archbishop of
Hamburg "potestatem constringendi omnes qui
illuc convenerint ad omnem justiciam faciendam[2]."
Market and fair were freeing themselves for judicial purposes from the direct control of the central
power, and by the 13th century the process was
complete. "In our presence," declared[3] Frederick
II. in 1218," judgment has been given by the princes
and magnates of our empire that if we have by
charter conferred on any one a fair or weekly market
the Count or other judge of that province has there no
jurisdiction or power of punishing offences." In Italy
and England the feudal lords had won the same
right of jurisdiction. " I grant and concede," says a
Neapolitan charter of 1115, "to the said monastery
and its abbots the rights of administering justice in
civil cases which may arise during the aforesaid
days" of the fair. As early as the 9th century a
monastery of Piacenza was granted the jurisdiction
over a newly founded fair, "homines quoque qui
ad ipsum mercatum occurrerint, si in aliquo devi-

---

[1] Keutgen, *Urkunden zur städtischen Verfassungsgeschichte*,
no. 39.

[2] *op. cit.*, no. 57.

[3] *op. cit.*, no. 66.

averint, a ministris ipsius monasterii distringantur et de transgressione justitiam perficiant[1]." In France not merely the jurisdiction over fairs but the right of founding them had passed into the hands of the feudal lords and it was not till the 13th century that the crown was able to recover the exclusive right of creating a new fair.

The second point that the early charters show is that the special protection of the merchant by the crown had been extended to all merchants on their journeys to and from market or fair. "They may found a public market," says the Meppen charter (946), " and those coming, returning and dwelling there shall have firm-stablished peace as our royal predecessors have long ago granted to the other public places of merchants." A special penalty safeguarded merchants and market. " By our imperial power," ran a clause in the Helsmarshauser charter (997)[2], "we ordain that all traders and others using the market, tarrying there or coming or returning, shall have such peace and such justice as those who trade at Mainz, Cologne and Dortmund, and those who infringe or disturb the market shall pay the same penalty."

From at least the 9th century onward the merchants were a class distinguished from the rest of the community by legal privileges that gave them a protection which others did not share, while market and fair formed a separate judicial unit which no royal judge could enter. From the very nature of the case this separate jurisdiction tended in the

---

[1] Pertile, *Storia del Diritto Italiano*, III. 505, note 373.
[2] Keutgen, *Urkunden*, no. 50 b.

absence of strong control from the central authority to adapt itself to the requirements of commerce and industry which in fair and market were the all-important elements. The establishment of isolated jurisdictions did not necessarily imply the employment of new law, but the gradual adoption of rules adapted to their special requirements was not only possible, but natural. The circumstances were favourable for the growth in market and fair of a special law for merchants and a special law arose. But it is not till the end of the 10th century when these favourable circumstances were well established that there is conclusive evidence that special rules existed.

The evidence of Notker and the reference to the customary law of the merchants of Tiel date from the commencement of the 11th century. Earlier evidence than this does not seem to exist. There is indeed a clause in the Bremen charter of 965 which may possibly refer to a special law for merchants —"negotiatores......potiantur jure quali ceterarum regalium institores urbium[1]." "Jure" however is an ambiguous term and may here only refer, as it often does elsewhere, to privileges such as freedom from toll or protection against violence. However this may be, special rules for deciding mercantile transactions existed in the 11th century and cannot be proved to exist earlier than the middle of the 10th[2] century.

---

[1] Keutgen, no. 7.

[2] Cf. case referred to by Huvelin, p. 194, and Sohm, *Die Entstehung des deutschen Städtewesen*, 54. The time is the reign of Charles the Bald. Two merchants have sold goods in common;

The rise of this special law coincided with the establishment of conditions highly favourable to the evolution of a special law for commerce. It is only natural to conclude that it is to these favourable conditions—the rise of local jurisdictions in markets and fairs free from the effective control of the central power and the existence of a merchant class distinct from the general mass of the population—that the origin of the Law Merchant is due.

In every country where commerce is of any importance the law must be adapted to the requirements of trade, but where the central power is strong and the judicial organisation uniform and under control, the adaptation need merely modify the common law of the land and need not create a separate system of law. In times and countries however where the central power is weak and the merchant and his disputes appear before courts secure from all effective control, the growth of a separate law may be expected. It does not seem too much to say that out of the immunity of market and fair courts rose the Law Merchant.

In the development of the Law Merchant the towns played an important, perhaps the most important part. The special law that had arisen in market

one of them receives payment and refuses to give the other his share. "Contentione oborta, judex fori E vocabulo, occurrit, cumque litem dirimere vellet, atque ille, qui pretium habuerat, compari se reddidisse omnibus modis affirmaret, nec dictis ejus fides adhiberetur, necessitate compulsus, dexteram contra basilicam extendens cum furo juramentum protulit." The case is curious, and it is difficult to decide whether we have here a special method of procedure.

and fair was transferred to the town. "If any dispute arise between my burghers," says the Freiburg charter[1] of 1120, "it shall not be decided according to my will or the will of their rector, but by the customary and legitimate law of all merchants and especially by the law of the merchants of Cologne." The Law Merchant became a part of the Law of the Town, and in Germany the theory has been advanced that in town law it was at first the all-important element from which the law of the town sprang[2]. According to this view the Law Merchant was the origin of town law, which was in its broad features merely an expansion and development of the special law of merchants. The theory has been disputed and for the early history of Law Merchant it is not of vital importance. It is sufficient that the Law Merchant became an integral part of the Law of the Town and of this fact there is no doubt. In every land during the 12th and following centuries the towns begin to record their laws and customs, which everywhere contain legal rules for commerce that differ from the common law of the land. For the development of the Law Merchant this reception of the law by the towns was of decisive importance. It was the period of the rise of towns to wealth and greatness and of the growth of their rights of self-government. The Law Merchant had now a wider sphere of activity. It was no longer confined to occasional fairs and markets but had found a permanent abode.

In the great commercial cities of Southern Europe

[1] Keutgen, no. 133, c. 5, p. 118.
[2] Sohm and others.

trade was now on a far vaster scale and far more complex than it had been in the fairs and markets of the 9th and 10th centuries ; and as commerce developed so did the Law Merchant. Everywhere the Law Merchant showed signs of progress, but in every country the progress was not the same. For in the main the development of the law was determined by the expansion of commerce and the growth of rights of self-government in the various cities, and these conditions were not satisfied everywhere to the same degree.

In Italy the cities of Lombardy and Tuscany were from the 11th century onward practically independent republics, while at the same time their trade advanced by leaps and bounds. The bulk of the trade between Europe and the East was in their hand ; they had their settlements in Constantinople and the Levant. There was here free scope for the rise of new customs and for the development of commercial law. The cities of Italy realised that commerce and industry were the sources of their power and wealth, and to increase commerce and industry was the main object of their policy. Their independent position gave them a free hand and enabled them to adopt those rules and regulations that seemed best adapted to the requirements of trade. Under these favourable circumstances commercial law developed rapidly. Rules and customs multiplied and it was soon found necessary to commit the old customary law to writing. More completely than elsewhere the Law Merchant in Italy ceased to be a purely customary law and began to change into a Lex Scripta. It was a great change, but it is easy to exaggerate both its completeness and its importance. The Law did not become a purely statutory law, for the commercial statutes made no claim to completeness. The force of old unrecorded customs was expressly recognised and new customs were constantly forming.

As original authorities for the early history of the Law Merchant the Italian commercial statutes are invaluable; they throw a flood of light upon the origin and development of commercial rules and customs that then or afterwards found their way into the commercial laws of Europe. So long as the Law Merchant remained a customary law, unwritten and unrecorded in statutes or codes, almost the only original sources were scattered references in charters and contemporary histories. But in neither charter nor historian is detailed information to be found. Their evidence is indeed sufficient to prove that a special law existed, but it is impossible from them alone to form a full and comprehensive view of what the rules and doctrines of the Law Merchant in early times really were. The rarity through Europe of early records of the fair and market courts makes the evidence of the Italian statutes all the more valuable. A striking feature of these Italian statutes is their length and completeness. The merchant gild regulations of Piacenza which run into several hundred paragraphs and the elaborate Pisan "constitutum usus" date in part from the 12th century. In no other country can be found such ample information of such early date upon the customs and regulations that prevailed among merchants. Nor do the Pisan and Piacenza laws stand alone. For the 13th and 14th centuries there exist, for almost every city of importance in Northern Italy collections of commercial statutes that give a full and detailed account of the commercial law that was observed within the city[1]. The history of their formation requires examination[2].

In most, though not in all of the Italian cities commercial law is to be found mainly in the statutes of the merchant gilds. In Italy, as elsewhere, the gilds were allowed a large measure of self-government and framed their own regulations, which merely required to be confirmed by the governing body of the city. These regulations were subject to constant revision and emendation, and in many of the gilds there were special and often permanent officials—the emendatores—whose duty it was to revise the statutes and suggest alterations. Their proposals needed to be confirmed by the general council of the gild and by the city authorities. It would be a mistake however to regard these regulations, in spite of their origin, as gild statutes pure and simple. Once confirmed, tacitly or expressly, they had all the authority of state law, binding upon all who traded within the city[3]. No doubt at first their application was limited to members of the gild, but, as will be

[1] v. Lattes, *Il Diritto Commerciale nella Legislazione Statuaria.*
[2] *op. cit.*, paragraph 4, pp. 57—70.
[3] Gild Statutes of Bergamo, cap. xxx. ''Magnifici Potestates et Rectores Pergami praesentes et futuri eorumque judices, aliique jus dicentes in Civitate Pergami residentes, necnon praefati Domini Consules qui praecedere debent et debebunt regimini

shown later, the gild judges gradually acquired jurisdiction over all persons actually engaged in trade
within the city, whether members of the gild or not.
As heads of the gild the "consules mercatorum"
administered the law, but the city magistrates were
under a strict obligation, to which they had to swear
on entering upon their office, to aid, if necessary, the
gild consuls with all the powers of the state in
securing the execution of their judicial sentences. In
Italy the Gild Merchant was in fact a subordinate
legislature for commercial purposes. It was not in
every Italian town however that the gild possessed this
important legislative authority. In Genoa for example
the commercial laws are to be sought in the ordinary
civil law of the city. But such cases are rare, and as
a general rule the main body of commercial laws is
in Italian towns contained in the statutes of the
Merchant Gild. The civil codes of the various cities
indeed contained commercial rules of law, but they
merely served to supplement the gild regulations[1].
In commercial matters the consuls decided in the
first place according to the statutes of the gild and
only referred to the common law in cases where the
gild had laid down no rule. Naturally Gild Law
and Common Law occasionally clashed, and the gild

dictae societatis Mercatorum Pergami teneantur, et debeant
executioni mandare omnia et singula statuta et ordinamenta
dictae Societatis ac Communitatis......et si quid actum sit in
contrarium, non valeat nec teneat ipso jure; *et dicta Statuta
habeant et teneant eandem vim, robur et firmitatem quam haberent
ac si facta forent per Consilium Generale Communis Pergami....*"

[1] Lattes, *op. cit.*, p. 71. Lattes' notes 4 and 5 give numerous
references.

statutes sometimes expressly declare that the rule of the gild should be observed, "notwithstanding any statute in the civil law to the contrary[1]."

In the earlier Italian statutes there is little trace of direct borrowing. Their general agreement upon main points is striking, but it was due not to imitation but to the fact that the statutes were everywhere based upon the customs of the merchants, which throughout Italy were much the same. In the 14th and 15th centuries, however, the Lombard towns began to borrow literally or with only slight verbal alterations from one another and, as a natural result, greater uniformity was introduced[2]. This borrowing and slavish imitation was not, as will be seen, confined to Italy, and in other countries it was practised on a far larger scale. In North-Western Europe the customs of one town were often transferred in their entirety, and this system was one of the chief causes that tended to maintain and to increase the general uniformity that characterized the Law Merchant.

The commercial statutes of Italy during the 12th, 13th and 14th centuries will well repay close study. Abounding in detail and regulating every branch of commerce, they provide information upon almost every point of interest. Subject to constant additions and modifications they trace clearly the lines along which commercial jurisprudence was developing: while, framed and fashioned as they were by the merchants themselves, they represent not so much

[1] Lattes, *Il Diritto Commerciale nella Legislazione Statuaria*, p. 75, note 10.

[2] *op. cit.*, p. 61, and notes 24—7.

M. 3

the law that the State thought best, as the law and customs that were approved by the merchant class. Moreover the early rise and rapid development of commerce in Italy gives a special value to Italian commercial legislation which on many points was in advance of that of other countries. It is in Italy that many of the rules of the Law Merchant had their origin, and it is in Italy that the Law Merchant first developed on a large scale from purely customary to statute law. From every point of view the Italian statutes are of the highest value as sources for the early history of the Law Merchant. Alone however they are altogether insufficient. The Law Merchant varied from country to country, it did not everywhere at the same time pass through the same stage of its development, and the law of every country showed occasional peculiarities that never found general acceptance. Consequently the existence of a commercial rule of law in the early statutes of Italy is no proof of itself that the rule was at that time generally recognised by the Law Merchant throughout Europe.

In Italy, for example, in the Middle Ages it was generally established that the mere possession of a bill containing an alternative clause to bearer—" tibi aut cui hoc scriptum in manu paruerit" or the like —was sufficient to establish a right to payment[1]. It would be hazardous however to conclude that this view was at that time held in all the trading centres

[1] Bruschellini, *Trattato dei Titoli al Portatore*, §§ 106 and 107 and note 198 : "il portatore di un titolo a clausola alternativa era legittimato ad otternere la prestazione senza che fosse in verun modo tenuto a dimostrare la legalità del suo possesso." In Southern France, *e.g.* Bearn, the rule held good in the 13th century.

of Europe. As a matter of fact there is good reason for believing that at that early period mere possession of such a bill was not everywhere regarded as sufficient of itself to secure payment[1]. While the Italian statutes present a fuller and more comprehensive treatment of early commercial law than is found elsewhere, they represent after all but one variety of the Law Merchant, and the laws and customs of the towns and seaports of France and Spain, England and Germany need to be examined and compared before a general view of the development of the early Law Merchant can be obtained.

In many ways the commercial laws of other countries were framed and developed under different conditions from those that prevailed in Italy. For while in Italy the law of each city was at first mainly of native growth, showing few signs of direct imitation of other city codes, in England, France and Germany the town custumals were broadly speaking based upon those of a few leading cities. The custumals of Lubeck, Magdeburg, Cologne, Frankfort and Soest were transferred to towns in every part of Germany, while in France Lorris served as a prototype for 300,

---

[1] Des Marez, *Lettres de Foires*, pp. 65—7. The customs of Malines declare "that no one can exact a debt as bearer of a letter, if he does not prove that he acts as bearer by procuration or cession of the person named in the obligation, although the obligation contains this clause: payable to the bearer of this letter. "Nyemant en *mach* scult heysschen als bringere des briefs, *tensij dat blijcke* dat hi procuratie oft transport heeft van den ghenen die in de obligatie principalijck genoempt ist, niettegenstaende dat obligatie inhoudt: te betalene den bringere des Briefs." Quoted by Des Marez, 67.

Beaumont for more than 500 towns. For its municipal laws Wales went to Hereford, Ireland to
Bristol or Breteuil, while Newcastle was one of the
principal sources of Scotch burghal law[1]. In
Germany the legal tie between parent and daughter
city was more closely maintained than in England
and France. The court of the German mother city
often served as a regular court of appeal from the
courts of the cities that had adopted its law. Of
these superior courts Lubeck, Magdeburg, Eisenach,
Frankfort and Iglau were the most important.
Many of the decisions of these courts have been
preserved, and in commercial cases their interpretation of the law is the more valuable in that it
declares the law not of a single city, but of numerous
towns scattered throughout Germany. The reports,
for example, of two cases decided in the courts of
Magdeburg and Iglau during the 14th century are
sufficient to establish for many towns in Bohemia
and Eastern Germany the legal effect in bills of an
alternative clause to bearer[2]. This system of affilia-
tion of town custumals supplied a unifying force
that was in early times absent in Italy. Nor is this
the only difference. The merchant gilds had not
elsewhere the same direct predominant influence
upon the formation of commercial law that the
Lombard and Tuscan gilds possessed. Almost everywhere they existed and often they exercised great
influence upon the town government, but outside

[1] Gross, *Gild Merchant*.

[2] Brunner, *Forschungen*, 655. (Zur Geschichte des Inhaber-
papiers in Deutschland.)

Italy their statutes are not so important, considered as sources of commercial law, as the town custumals. Differing largely in bulk and importance from place to place these custumals cannot, with the exception of two or three famous collections of maritime laws, be in any sense considered as commercial codes. Criminal law and administrative details as a rule occupy far more space than purely commercial rules. Still, owing to the lack of other sources, they are often the only authorities available for determining the law that governed commercial transactions within the cities.

The Law Merchant moreover was not everywhere free, as it was to all intents and purposes free in Italy, from the control and influence of external authorities. In England Edward I. changed the law observed in markets and fairs, and in both England and Germany the town custumals required the confirmation of the Lord of the town. Appeals could be made in France from the courts of the great fairs of Champagne to the Parlement of Paris and in England to the Chancellor and Council under the Statute of Staple. Still, though the conditions were not everywhere equally favourable in every country, the town served as a centre for the development of the Law Merchant, for in the towns of every country the essential condition necessary for its development was present. During the 12th and 13th centuries the practical independence of the great commercial cities of Europe was, no doubt, almost unique in Europe, but "everywhere the separation of the town courts from the ordinary courts of the land had been introduced in England and Scandinavia, no less than on the Continent[1]." It was in fair and market and town that the Law Merchant was created and developed, and it is in the records of fair and market, of town and seaport, that the sources for its history mainly lie.

[1] Hegel, *Städte und Gilder der germanischen Völker im Mittelalter*, II. 506.

CHAPTER III.

THE COURTS OF THE LAW MERCHANT.

In the 10th and 11th centuries, when the Law Merchant was in process of formation, the only courts that could in any sense be regarded as special courts for commercial purposes were held in markets and fairs. But as the independence of the towns increased and their commerce expanded, there were gradually created in some of the great cities of Southern Europe permanent courts distinct from mere market or fair courts, with a jurisdiction confined to cases of a commercial character. The origin of these courts is due to the power, independence and commercial activity of the town; and in those countries where the central authority was strong and commerce important, the forces that created the local commercial court tended to create courts with commercial jurisdiction for the whole land. This is however a late development, for it was but slowly that the central authority became powerful enough to enforce a uniform system of judicial organisation, and even when it had the power it did not always see the necessity of establishing separate courts of commerce. It was especially for maritime law that the central power felt the necessity of special jurisdiction, and in France and England, for example, the special local courts that had long existed in seaport and harbour were but the forerunners of the Admiralty, a national court with a general jurisdiction in maritime cases. It was not everywhere that commercial courts arose ; in most European towns commercial cases were tried in the ordinary town court, which possessed jurisdiction in both civil and criminal matters. Apart from purely maritime courts which are found in many parts of Europe, it was mainly in Southern Europe where commercial activity was most intense that special courts gradually arose with jurisdiction limited to trade disputes. As in many other branches of commercial law, Italy led the way.

The rise of commercial courts is in Italy closely connected with the development of the city consti-tution. By the end of the 11th century many of the cities had won practical independence and the powers of administration and justice had passed into the hands of their own magistrates. Upon these magistrates lay the whole burden of the administra-tion of the city republic. In each city their number was very small and, as in the case of the early Roman consuls, there was no division of functions: they were judges as well as administrators. Natu-rally as the towns grew and commerce expanded the burden proved too heavy, and during the course of the 12th century special magistrates[1]—consules

[1] Pertile, *Storia del Diritto Italiano*, II. i. 41, note 49.

judices—were appointed in several towns of Northern Italy. They were not, it is true, in any sense commercial judges, but their creation shows that the old system was inadequate, and partly explains the rapid rise of the aldermen of the merchant gild to importance as commercial judges. For it is only a few years later (1154) that the first notice of the "consules mercatorum" appears; and by the end of the century their existence can be proved in most of the cities of Northern Italy[1]. As heads of the Merchant Gilds these consuls exercised a general control over the members of the gild, which included all or practically all the traders within the town. In addition to political and administrative duties they began to judge commercial cases in which members of the gild were involved, and their court gradually developed from a mere Gild court with jurisdiction only over its own members into a commercial court with jurisdiction over all the cases of a mercantile character that were likely to arise within the city.

In the early gild statutes the jurisdiction of the consuls is limited to the merchants of the city and foreign traders, and the Statutes of Brescia (1313) add the significant definition, "et ille intelligatur mercator qui publice exercet mercathendiam et qui scriptus sit sua spontanea voluntate." Similarly the statutes of Como (1281) give jurisdiction to the consuls over merchants, but add, "merchants are

---

[1] Lattes, *op. cit.*, p. 39, note 1, gives very numerous references. For their general importance see Pertile II. part i. p. 196 and notes.

understood to be those who are or shall be of the merchant gild of Como." It must also be noticed that the jurisdiction of the gild, even over its own members, was not at first of an obligatory character. A member of the gild was within his rights if he summoned a fellow-member before the ordinary civil court of the city instead of submitting the dispute to the decision of the consuls of the gilds. It was however a right that the merchants rarely wished, and still less rarely dared, to exercise. For in the first place legal proceedings were far less expeditious and consequently far more costly in the city than in the gild court. An even more effective reason however was the firm determination of the gild to uphold its jurisdiction over its own members in commercial cases[1]. Under the severest penalties it forbade its members to appeal, in cases where they alone were concerned, to any court save that of the gild. As a last resource the gild did not hesitate to expel members who ignored its claims to jurisdiction, and to forbid trade or intercourse with them. In the same spirit it often compelled foreign merchants as soon as they came to reside in the city to swear to

---

[1] *Statuto dell' Arte di Calimala dell' anno* 1301 (edited by Filippi), II. c. 38. "Quia facta mercatorum qui inter eos aguntur convenientius tractari possunt coram consulibus artium sub quibus resident litigantes quam coram aliis judicibus, provisum est *quod nulla persona de arte Kallismale possit vel debeat extra curiam consulum Kallismale traere vel convenire aliquam personam que teneatur sub dicta arte Kallismale* in judicio in quo tracteretur vel (word wanting) questio fieret vel moveretur de mercantia mutuo deposito vel cambio vel *alia re ex mercantia descendente* SUB PENA a contrafaciente tollenda ARBITRIO CONSULUM Kallismale."

submit to the jurisdiction of the consuls. Thus, while the jurisdiction of the gild was in theory only concurrent with that of the ordinary civil courts of the city, over its own members and over foreign merchants it was in practice almost exclusive. By the 15th century its claim to exclusive jurisdiction over the commercial transactions of merchants had in many places been acknowledged by the State. At Mantua and Bergamo, for example, the city magistrates were forbidden under the penalty of a heavy fine to interfere in any way with the juris- diction of the consuls of the gild[1].

Gradually moreover the gild court acquired jurisdiction over non-members. During the course of the 14th and 15th century anyone who carried

---

[1] A.D. 1400. *Lo Statuto dell' Università Maggiore dei Mercanti in Mantova* (edited by Portioli), cap. 41. "Item statuimus...quod *nullus officialis* civitatis Mantuae aut ejus districtus de cetero audeat vel *presumat, aliqualiter, se intromittere de iis quae spectant et pertinent ad jurisdictionem, decisionem,* terminationem et cognitionem *dictorum consulum.* Attenta concessione decretorum et ordinamentorum dictis consulibus indultorum et attributorum *neque ipsorum jurisdictionem quomodolibet impedire....*"

A.D. 1429. *Statute della Mercanzia di Brescia* (edited by Crotta), cap. 44. "Ordinatum est quod D. Potestas Brixiae, prae- sens et futuri, caeterique officiales nullatenus debeant, sive possint impedire consules Mercantiae Brixiae nec eorum officium, quin possint et valeant juxta statuta in praesenti volumine procedere, et jus unicuique facere, neque possint aliqualiter intromittere de spectantibus et pertinentibus officio praefatorum D. consulum ; immo teneantur et debeant, ipsis D. consulibus requirentibus, omne auxilium et favorem pro dicto eorum officio exercendo tam in civitate quam in districtu Brixiae dare et praestare......et quicquid actum fuerit contra praedicta non valeat nec teneat ipso jure...."

on trade, whether member of a gild or not, came to
be regarded from a legal point of view as a merchant
and was subject to the jurisdiction of the consuls.
The gild statutes of Brescia of the year 1313, for
example, only admit the jurisdiction of the consuls
over merchants who had been enrolled as members
of the gild, while the statutes of 1429 add, "etiam
illi qui veniunt vel uti faciant stratas mercantiarum
cum ipsis mercantiis et negotiationibus[1]." At
Florence[2] the city statutes (1415) expressly recognised the competence of the various gild courts
to deal with complaints against non-members,
provided that firstly the defendant did not belong to
any of the other gilds and was a "civis, comitatinus
vel destrictualis florentinus," that is, was a private
citizen, not a merchant, and secondly that the dispute
related to a matter pertaining to one of the gilds.
A few years earlier (1393) they had already secured
legal recognition of their jurisdiction over all those
actually engaged in trade or industry, whether they
were members of the gild or not. At Venice about
the same time there was a dispute between the gild
and the city authorities as to whether the transactions of bankers with their private customers were
under the jurisdiction of the gild consuls; and finally

[1] 1429. St. Merc. of Brescia, cap. 43. In case of doubt as to
the competence of consuls, the consuls and merchants were to
settle the question of competence: "et si quod dubium oriretur,
stetur declarationi praefatorum D. consulum cum quattuor ex
mercatoribus publice utentibus, vel uti facientibus, stratas supra-
scriptas cum mercimoniis vel negotiationibus."

[2] Lastig, *Entwickelungswege und Quellen des Handelsrechts*,
p. 334 and note 2.

the question was settled in favour of the gild. Everywhere in Italy the jurisdiction of the gild court was extending, and by the middle of the 15th century it may fairly be regarded as a special court for commercial cases[1]. The development however was not in every town complete; for in some cities the gild court still retained criminal jurisdiction over its own members and cannot consequently be considered as a purely commercial court. In many towns, on the other hand, it was expressly declared that even when only its own members were concerned the gild court had merely the right to decide cases of a commercial nature.

Of Italian commercial courts the Pisan Curia Maris[2] is especially interesting, as an early example of a purely maritime tribunal of far earlier date than the more famous Consulad del Mare of Barcelona, while its history shows the opposition that the gild courts experienced from the ordinary courts and the city magistrates. In the 12th century there were several courts in Pisa, the most important of which were the "curia legis" and the "curia usus." The latter had jurisdiction in commercial and maritime cases. But just as the gild consuls in other Italian towns developed into commercial judges, the consuls of the great Sea Gild of Pisa, the "ordo maris," after a long and severe struggle obtained sole jurisdiction and freedom from the control of other courts in all

[1] For the extent of jurisdiction of consular courts see Lattes, p. 81 and notes 6, 7, 8, and pp. 251—3 with the notes.

[2] For Pisan Sea consulate see Schaube, *Das Consulat des Meeres in Pisa*, of which I have made great use.

cases of a maritime character. It was only gradually that the city recognised their claims to jurisdiction. In the city statutes of 1233 they were only recognised as "in loco judicum" and were forbidden to decide any cases that came within the Province of the "curia legis." The old jurisdiction of the "curia usus" still remained and was in maritime cases concurrent with that of the sea consuls, whose sentences moreover were still subject to appeal. It would seem that it was only with great difficulty that the maritime court acquired the right of deciding cases finally and irrevocably, for the gild found it necessary to bind its consuls by an oath to do all in their power to procure a law limiting the right of appeal from its court. In a revision of the city laws (1281) their demand was allowed and the right of appeal limited, but it was not till sixty years later that all decisions of the court were recognised by the republic as final and irrevocable. The jurisdiction of the court was extensive, and by the middle of the 14th century covered all cases of a maritime nature. The consuls were entitled[1] to take cognisance of all disputes relating to freights and consignments, and loans and commercial documents connected with maritime trade, and all questions of profits, losses, average and wages, that might arise. Nor are the judicial powers of the consuls less extensive if regarded from the point of view of the persons over whom the consuls were authorised to exercise jurisdiction. That their jurisdiction extended not only over merchants, but also over ship-builders and

[1] Schaube, 32—3. Breve ordinis Maris, 2.

carpenters, caulkers, sail, and rope-makers and oakum workers, is not of itself surprising for their connection with the shipping industry is obvious. But the inclusion, among the persons subject to the consular jurisdiction, of joiners, chest-makers, painters, coopers, potters and sadlers, would seem to show that the court was not a purely maritime court. In all probability, however, it would be erroneous to assume that the court exercised jurisdiction over these classes of persons in all cases. Only when they were involved in disputes of a maritime character would they appear before the court of the sea gild. Their inclusion in the list would seem to show that, as in other Italian towns, the competence of the gild court still partly depended upon the profession or trade of the suitors, and that to secure jurisdiction in all cases which were actually of a maritime character the gild found it advisable to procure the insertion of such artisans as joiners, chest-makers and coopers in the list of those who by virtue of their personal occupation were subject to the jurisdiction of the consuls. In the ordinary commercial courts as well as in the maritime courts the test of the Court's competence became gradually less and less a personal test, and the nature of the dispute became more important. But the process was not complete, and at the close of the Middle Ages it was necessary in Italian commercial courts that one at least of the suitors, most often the defendant, must belong by profession to one of the trading or industrial classes regarded as personally subject to the consular jurisdiction. That the personal test had ceased in practice to be of any importance was not so much because the theory had changed as that all classes who were actually engaged in individual or mercantile pursuits were gradually recognised as personally within the jurisdiction of the gild court, and that consequently the occupation or profession of the suitors could rarely be raised as an objection to the exercise of the court's authority. It should also be noticed that any objection to the competence of the court should in Pisa, as in most other Italian cities, be made at an early stage of the proceeding; and objections made later, even if otherwise valid, are expressly excluded by the statutes[1]. It is interesting to note that the creation of the Pisan "consules maris" and of the English Court of Admiralty was probably due to the same cause. Schaube has shown for Pisa, and Marsden for England, that the creation of a special jurisdiction for maritime disputes was in all probability due to a desire to keep within due bounds the piratical proclivities of English and Pisan sailors. In England the king was obliged to pay large sums of money as compensation to foreign merchants whose ships had been plundered by English subjects, while at Pisa trade declined and frequent disputes arose for the same reason.

In view of the great importance that the sea consulate acquired in later times, especially in Spain,. it seems necessary to lay stress upon the fact that the Pisan court is of earlier date than any similar institution that existed elsewhere. First mentioned

[1] Schaube, 141.

in a document of the year 1201 and probably not in existence in the preceding year, the Pisan sea consuls obtained from the State an acknowledgement of their judicial powers, as early as 1233[1]. For no other Italian or Spanish city is there satisfactory evidence that at that date maritime consuls existed with judicial functions. In Spain the Sea Consulate of Valencia is the earliest, but it goes back no further than 1283. Sea consuls are indeed found in Genoa early in the 13th century (1206), but they possessed no powers of jurisdiction: they were custom house officials, not judges, and within a hundred years their title of sea consuls had changed into the more appropriate name of "collectors[2]." It was long thought that earlier instances of the sea consuls existed in Amalfi and Trani, but the evidence is far from conclusive. The maritime code of Amalfi, the Latin redaction of which may possibly date from the 12th century, though the Italian version is as late as the end of the 14th or the commencement of the 15th century, certainly contains references in both the Latin and Italian redactions to consuls, but nowhere are sea consuls mentioned[3]. Schaube suggests with great probability that the consuls of the Latin version are the ship consuls that the merchant vessels of the early Middle Ages often carried, and that on the other hand it is quite possible that the consuls of the Italian version correspond to the sea consuls of Pisa, as they are

[1] Schaube, 4—6 and 14—15.
[2] Schaube, 232.
[3] Schaube, 276. Wagner, *Seerecht*, 62.

often mentioned in the plural and their judicial functions, so far as they are mentioned, are of a maritime character. According to this view, if sea consuls did exist in Amalfi, there is no proof of their existence earlier than the 14th century. To Trani[1] sea consuls have been assigned as early as the middle of the 12th century, for this is the date given for the Trani maritime code in its 16th century Italian translation. The Latin original of the code, however, is not extant, and it is possible that as Pardessus suggests the date 1063 is a mistake for 1363 : Schaube indeed is inclined to place the code as late as the middle of the 15th century. The evidence would seem to show that to Pisa belongs the credit of creating an institution that in the following centuries was to exercise a vast influence upon the development of maritime law in Europe.

The Italian system was not confined to Italy. Trading and settled in every part of Europe the Italian merchants carried as far as possible their institutions with them to their new abode. Accustomed as they were in Italy to be judged in commercial cases not by the civil judges but by the consuls of the merchant gild, they preferred to be judged when abroad by a fellow-merchant according to their own laws. It was one of the most characteristic maxims of the municipal laws of medieval times that the citizens residing abroad should whenever possible seek justice before judges of their

---

[1] Schaube, 277—9. Wagner, *Seerecht*, 61. "Die angegebene Entstehungszeit des (lateinischen) Originals muss aus verschiedenen Gründen bezweifelt werden." Cf. note 3 of Wagner where Sclopis, Capasso and Pertile are cited as accepting the date 1363.

own nationality. Rarely during the Middle Ages would an Italian merchant cite a fellow-citizen before a foreign tribunal; all disputes between citizens of the same Italian town were in foreign cities settled as a general rule by consuls elected by the merchants themselves or appointed direct by the home authorities[1]. "All those," declares a Pisan Law of the 12th century, "who without our bounds are elected captains by the consuls or a public agent, or by the merchants residing there when there is no captain appointed by the consuls or agent, shall be considered "loco judicum." It was by no means necessary that the number of merchants resident in the foreign city should be large. The Placentian statutes (c. 1200), for example, considered three sufficient. These foreign consuls fall into three classes : the "consules missi," the "consules electi" and the "consules hospites." In many great towns, especially those of

[1] Goldschmidt, 181, n. 143 cites (13th century) out of Statutes of the consules placitorum of Genoa, "Laudabo publice in parlamento quod nullus Janue appellet aliquem vel aliquos Januenses ad extraneum judicem vel extraneam curiam," except "quando Janue consulatus fortasse in ea terra non esset," and gives many other references.

Cf. for Germany Stadtrecht of Soest (1130—1150) cap. 29 in Keutgen, No. 139, p. 141. "Item constitutum est quod si concives nostri extra provinciam inter se dissenserint, non se ad extranea trahant judicia; aut vel inter se litem componant, vel, si tot sunt personae, judicem unum de consociis judicem statuant qui litem si potest sopiat : si non potest, causam, donec ad propria redeant, differant. Hoc constitutum, si quis infregerit, x m. et carratam vini vadiabit." The Soest custumal served as model for many other towns. Stadtrecht Münster Bielefeld (c. 1221), cap. 30, Keutgen, p. 152. "Qui suum civem alibi traxerit in judicium, vadiabit ii S."

Eastern Europe, the most important cities, such as Venice, Genoa and Pisa, had obtained the concession of one of the town quarters for their merchants. The importance of these settlements may be judged from the fact that in the year 1170 no fewer than 20,000 Venetians left Italy upon the Emperor Manuel's invitation to settle in the cities of the Byzantine Empire, and that when war broke out between Venice and the Eastern Empire in the following year 10,000 Venetians were seized in Constantinople alone[1]. To administer justice and exercise a general control in these outlying settlements the Italian city appointed "consules missi." As officials independent of the local sovereign and yet exercising jurisdiction over a permanent and often numerous group of foreign residents, the consuls naturally seriously limited the power and authority of the local courts, and they were only nominated in cases where the Italian city had been able to persuade the local sovereign by treaty to waive his full rights of jurisdiction. The consules electi differed from the consules missi in that they were elected by the merchants of the colony and as a rule were to be found in the smaller settlements and towns of Western Europe, while the consules missi were only found in large and important colonies and especially in those situated in the East. It would seem that in the great fairs of Champagne the various Italian cities were not only represented for judicial and administrative purposes by consuls

[1] Giesebrecht, *Die Zeit Kaiser Friedrichs des Rotbarts* I. pp. 678—9.

of their own, but that all the Italian merchants of
Northern Italy formed a union subject to the jurisdiction of the " Capitaneus " or consul of the union.
There are numerous references[1] to this official, and
that his authority was considerable is shown by the
statutes of the Calimala Gild of Florence. For while
the special consuls of the Florentine gilds in France
had only the right to inflict penalties to the value of
40 shillings, they were instructed to execute the
judgments of the " Capitano de' Lombardi," whose
power to inflict penalties of unlimited amount is
expressly recognised. Outside France however there
are no traces of a union of the Italian cities for
judicial purposes, and the " Captain of the Lombards "
in the Champagne fairs seems to be the only judge
recognised in common by the independent cities of
Italy during the Middle Ages. In the Italian
consular system lies the origin of the commercial
consul of modern times; and the consules missi, in
particular, form an interesting parallel with the
modern European consuls in the Turkish Empire
and the far East. Both exercise jurisdiction over
their compatriots, both are appointed by the home

---

[1] Goldschmidt, 195—199, Stat. Calimalae (Florence 1301),
Lb. iv. rubric 8. " Consules Francie (*i.e.* the Florentine consuls
in France) habeant potestatem reddendi jura et cognoscendi de
causis usque ad libr. x. turnenses. Item habeant potestatem
imponendi usque ad s. xl. cuique et quotiens voluerint pro eorum
offitio et ipsam penam auferre. Verum si quod preceptum fecerint
alicui de voluntate *consulum societatis lombardorum* tunc possint
imponere et tollere penam et penas usque ad libr. 50 *et plus eorum
arbitrio.*" In the Italian redaction of the Statutes of 1332, Lb. i.
rubric 11, the phrase is " di volontà del capitano de' Lombardi."

government and both owe their judicial powers to a special agreement between the two countries.

The "consul hospes[1]," on the other hand finds his historical counterpart in the Greek "proxenos." Like the Greek official the "consul hospes" was a citizen of the state in which the merchants under his protection resided, and his tenure of office, like that of the "proxenos," was permanent and not for a limited time as was that of all other Italian consuls. There is however one essential point of difference between the Greek and the medieval official. The "consul hospes" was not only the protector of the merchants of the city which nominated him, he was also their judge, while the "proxenos" of ancient Greece had no judicial powers. "The proxenos," says Schaube, "was the patron of his protégés before all the authorities and before the tribunal; the consul hospes is himself the judge of those who have been recommended to him; the town which nominates him confers upon him the jurisdiction; the town in which he exercises his functions authorises their exercise within its territory in recognition of the principle of personal law and also because the judge depends upon the town itself in his capacity as citizen, and as such is in a relation of close subordination to the local government." In all probability, as Morel has pointed out, the consul hospes furthered in no small measure the adoption by other countries of the principles of Italian commercial law. As citizen of

[1] v. Morel, *Les Juridictions Commerciales au Moyen Age*, 84—88. Schaube, *La proxénie au Moyen Age*. Revue du droit international et de législation comparée, 1896.

the one country and judge of the merchants of the other he served as a link that connected the legal system of both.

Almost everywhere the development of commercial tribunals in Italy followed the same line of progress, and it would seem that in that development the two main factors were the spirit of liberty and the identity of the interests of the city with the interests of commerce. In commerce the Italian cities of the Middle Ages lived and moved and had their being. Almost every citizen was an artizan or merchant and almost every merchant or artizan was a citizen. The rights and privileges of self-government in municipal matters taught the citizen to aspire to self-government in his capacity as merchant and trained him to exercise those rights wisely when once they had been granted, while the identity of the interests of commerce with the prosperity of the city encouraged the city authorities to grant a considerable latitude of self-government and of judicial functions to the merchants and artisans who formed the mainstay of the State. Strikingly is the spirit of liberty evident in the free combination of the merchants in the merchant gild and in their willing submission to the jurisdiction of the consuls and their avoidance of the city courts. Through the loyalty of the merchant to the head of his gild was slowly evolved the merchant judge, whose authority the State had finally only to confirm, not to create.

In the history of the Spanish courts of commerce the chief point of interest is the rise of maritime courts of the type of the Pisan sea consulate. In Spain, the sea consuls were, as in Pisa, maritime judges with full powers of jurisdiction over all maritime disputes. At Barcelona there was a curious reversal of the process of development that took place at Pisa, where from the "Curia Usus"—a court with jurisdiction both for maritime and ordinary commercial disputes—were gradually wrested all maritime cases, which were transferred to the consulate of the sea. The Barcelona consulate, on the other hand, originally created as a purely maritime court, finally developed into a court which took cognisance of all commercial cases of whatever nature.

As similar courts of a later date than the Pisan consulate the Spanish maritime courts naturally suggest the theory that they were founded in direct imitation of the Pisan institution. There is much that supports the theory. It was in the Aragonese kingdom that the sea consulate in Spain first arose, and the commercial connection between Aragon and Pisa was permanent and close. As early as 1233 James I. of Aragon granted trading privileges in the Balearic Islands to Pisan merchants; and a few years later (1256) he granted permission to the Pisans in every part of his kingdom to elect consuls and be judged according to their own law in all cases, even those of bloodshed. About the same time (1278) the Catalonians had their consuls and rectors in Pisa, and the king of Aragon declared (1284) it was his intention "always to honour the Pisans as they have ever been honoured by our predecessors."

Schaube[1], who has gathered and marshalled all the available evidence, holds that the close commercial connection between Pisa and the Aragonese kingdom and the striking similarity that existed between the sea consulate in the two States justifies the belief that there was in Spain direct imitation of the Pisan court. On the other hand Goldschmidt, whose opinion is of the greatest weight, does not consider the theory proved, though he lays stress repeatedly on the influence of Pisan upon Spanish maritime law. The evidence however adduced by Schaube is so strong that his theory may be regarded as in the highest degree probable.

It is for Valencia, at the time already part of the Aragonese kingdom, that there is the earliest evidence of the existence of a sea consulate. Its creation (1283) was due to royal charter. Every year two consuls were to be elected by the "probi homines maris" and confirmed by the king. Just as at Pisa the consuls were elected by the sea gild, they were in Valencia elected by the "good men of the sea," and in Valencia as in Pisa the consuls were laymen, skilled "in the art and usage of the sea." But while in the Italian city the sea consuls also possessed administrative functions, in Valencia their powers were solely judicial. The law that they administered was the customary law of Barcelona. "They shall decide," runs a clause of the charter, "contracts and disputes between men of the sea and merchants, which are to be decided according to the custom of the sea as it was wont

[1] Schaube, *Das Consulat des Meeres in Pisa*, 239—241.

to be done at Barcelona." In the following year
(1284) a judgè of appeal was created whose nomination the king reserved to himself. The king however
only once exercised his right of nomination, and the
election of the judge of appeal lay, as did that of the
consuls, in the hands of the "navigators, masters and
mariners." The jurisdiction of the court was extensive. "The consuls," declare the regulations of the
court (1336—43)[1], "determine all questions which
concern freight, damage to cargo laden on board ship,
mariners' wages, partnerships in shipbuilding, sales
of ships, jettison, commissions entrusted to masters
or to mariners, debts contracted by the master who
has borrowed money for the wants or necessities of
his vessel, promises made by a master to a merchant,
or by a merchant to a master, goods found on the
open sea or on the beach, the fitting out of ships,
galleys, or other vessels, and generally all other contracts which are set forth in the customs of the sea."
"The consuls of the sea have all ordinary jurisdiction
over all the contracts which have to be determined
according to the custom and usage of the sea, and
which are declared, stated and specified in the
customs of the sea." Perhaps the most interesting
feature of the Valencian court was the influence
exercised by the mariners and merchants upon the
jurisdiction of the court and the law administered by
the consuls. This influence was not merely due to
the fact that the consuls were themselves merchants
or mariners elected in open assembly by the seamen

---

[1] *Black Book of Admiralty.*

and merchants of the town. In cases where there were reasonable grounds for suspecting the impartiality of the consul or the judge of appeal, the regulations provided that a prudhomme of the sea gild should be associated with them, and in the same spirit the consuls were ordered to take counsel with the prudhommes of the merchants and of the sea, should any doubt arise as to. what the law on any point really was. "When one of the consuls, or both, in any matter are objected to as suspected by either of the parties who proceed before them and the reasons of the suspicion are apparent, they have to associate with them a prudhomme of the gild of navigators, if one only of the consuls is objected to, and if both are objected to, they have to associate with them two prudhommes of the gild of navigators who are not suspected by the parties. And together with these they conduct the proceedings and give sentence in the matter." "The judge in the same way, if he is objected to on suspicion, has to. associate with him a prudhomme of the sea gild who is not suspected by either party." "The sentences which are given by the said consuls and judge are given according to the written customs of the sea and in accordance with what is declared in the different chapters of them. And there where the customs and chapters are not sufficient, they give them upon consultation with the prudhommes of the merchants and of the sea, that is, always according to the majority of the voices in council, regard being had to the persons who give their advice." It was not however only in cases of doubt or of suspected

partiality on the part of the consuls that the prudhommes of the sea or merchant gild were consulted.
In every case the opinion of the prudhommes was
taken. If a sentence was to be given "upon a
demand in writing," the "consuls with their scribe
proceed to the prudhommes of the merchants and
cause to be read before them the pleadings and
proceedings in the matters and take thereupon the
advice of the said prudhommes of the merchants.
Afterwards they take counsel of the prudhommes
of the sea...and sometimes they consult the prudhommes of the sea in the first place as it is most
convenient to them.   And if the advice of the two
bodies is in accordance, they give sentence in the
matter.   And if their advice is not in accordance...
they may confer together; and in case the prudhommes of the sea do not agree with the prudhommes
of the merchants, or will not confer with them, the
consuls may give their sentence according to the
advice of the prudhommes of the sea, for contracts
are to be determined according to the advice of the
latter and not according to the advice of the prudhommes of the merchants, if they do not wish so."
Similarly in cases of appeal the judge takes "counsel
upon the pleadings of the appeal both with the
prudhommes of the merchants and the prudhommes
of the sea; not with those who have given their
advice on the principal pleadings, but with others
in the manner above declared."   Evidently maritime
law in Valencia, and probably also in Barcelona from
whence Valencia originally took its law, had by the
middle of the fourteenth century become to a large

extent a written law[1]; but in the interpretation of
that written law and in the judicial recognition of
old usages or new unwritten customs, the judges were
bound to take the advice of the merchants and
seamen of the port, and the influence that seamen
and merchants so exercised upon the development of
the law it is hard to overestimate.

The procedure of the court at first allowed of
long delays, but a royal ordinance of the year 1336
ordering the consuls to administer speedy justice was
shortly followed by "the judicial order of the courts
of the consuls of the sea" which established a
summary procedure similar to that already adopted
in the gild courts of Italy[2]. "The consuls," the
regulation declares, "under charter of our lord the
king have power to hear the plaints and questions
which are brought before them and to determine
them duly, briefly and summarily and forthwith,
without the noise or formality of a judgment, sola
facti veritate attenta, that is to say, looking solely to
the truth of the facts, according as has been accustomed to be done after the usage and custom of the
sea." The summary procedure of the Valencian
court was adopted by the consular courts that later
on arose in other parts of the Aragonese kingdom,
and also by the English Admiralty Courts[3]. The
importance of the regulations of the Valencian court
and the influence they exercised upon the constitution and procedure of late Spanish courts is shown

---

[1] Wagner, *Seerecht*, 57—59.

[2] Schaube, *op. cit.* 245, regulations, c. 36.

[3] *Black Book of Admiralty.* Editor's note.

by the fact that they were placed as an introduction at the commencement of the famous Barcelona code of maritime law and that they were applied to the later consular courts of Spain.

From Valencia the sea consulate of Majorca took its form and constitution, for in the year 1343 Peter the Fourth of Aragon by a charter, the text of which is found in a printed collection of Perpignan charters, authorised the consuls of Majorca[1] to conform to the Valencian "judicial order." In the charter it was expressly stated that "the men of the sea shall assemble every year and elect a consul and judge from among (de) the men of the sea gild who shall determine and decide all cases which arise from maritime transactions." As in Pisa, the jurisdiction of the gild court met with strong opposition. The town government overrode the royal charter and, claiming the right to appoint the consuls and judge of appeal, appointed men who were not connected with maritime pursuits. The king seems to have sided at first with the municipal authorities and to have appointed for life the town clerk as scribe to the consuls. The gild protested and the king gave way, declaring that it was not his intention to act contrary to the charter of 1343.

Only a few years after the institution of the consulate at Majorca a royal charter granted to the sea consuls of Barcelona the rights of jurisdiction that the consuls in the former place possessed. The charter did not create sea consuls at Barcelona, for they existed before and perhaps long before the date

---

[1] Pardessus, *Collection de Lois Maritimes*, v. 325. Schaube, 246.

when the charter (1347) was granted, though the earliest certain reference to sea consuls in Barcelona goes no further than 1302, and it is doubtful whether they at that time possessed judicial powers. One important difference the charter established between the consulate at Barcelona and the consulate of Majorca or Valencia. In the latter the election of consuls and judge was in the hands of the sea gild, while at Barcelona their election was entrusted to the town authorities. The consuls were however brought into close touch with the merchants and seamen of the town by a royal ordinance (1394) which conferred on the consuls the right[1] to summon assemblies of the merchants and consuls with them on matters of commercial interest; at the same time an elective committee of from ten to twenty merchants was created and the committee and consuls were entrusted with administrative functions; " procurandi manutenendi et defendendi ubique artem mercantilem." A few years later (1401) a most important change took place. The consulate ceased to be a purely maritime tribunal and was granted by royal charter jurisdiction in "all civil cases arising out of mercantile transactions whether by land or by sea." As in Pisa, it was with difficulty that the Barcelona court made good its claim to pronounce final irrevocable sentences; and in 1405, for example, the freedom of the consulate from the control of royal courts was seriously endangered.

Appeals were allowed in cases of " restitutio in integrum," and delay or denial of justice through the

[1] Schaube, 252.

malice or negligence of the judges. Though a serious blow to the power of the consuls, who had urged that in cases that came within their jurisdiction no royal official could in any way interfere, the change was not permanent and a royal charter four years later recognised the claims of the consuls[1].

Gradually the sea consulate was established in the chief commercial towns of Spain, and by the middle of the 17th century it existed in Tortosa, Burgos, Bilbao, Seville and Madrid. Nor was the influence of the establishment of the sea consulate as a recognised institution in the Aragonese kingdom confined to Spain alone. It exercised a great influence in Sicily, Italy and France. At the close of the 13th century, when the royal house of Aragon obtained possession of Sicily and Southern Italy, the consulate, perhaps owing to Pisan influence, was already established in Messina, but under the new dynasty the powers and jurisdiction of the sea consuls at Messina increased[2]. They acquired by the commencement of the 14th century the right to nominate the consuls in foreign cities of all the towns of Sicily and, as at Barcelona, they finally obtained by royal charter (1450) jurisdiction over commercial cases of whatever nature. In all probability this change was due to the influence of the development that the sea consulate had undergone in Aragon. Similarly the political union of Southern Italy with Spain was followed by the almost universal establishment of the sea consulate in the ports of the kingdom of

[1] Pardessus, v. 481—4.
[2] Schaube, 274—5.

Naples. For France Perpignan, the capital of the county of Roussillon, served as the starting point of Spanish influence upon the creation and constitution of the sea consulate[1]. As early as 1388 King John of Aragon "granted to the town of Perpignan the right to have a sea consulate of the form regulated by the charter for Barcelona." " The Perpignan charter," says Pardessus," conferred upon the town the right to establish the consulate and authorised the magistrate to follow the rules relating to competence and procedure traced in the series of 42 articles in use at Valencia." Upon the acquisition of Roussillon by Louis XI. the judicial powers of the sea consuls of Montpelier, who " until then as simple aediles and subordinate administrative officials had been simply charged with the maintenance and super-intendence of the canal and port," were reorganised upon the model of the sea consulate of Perpignan. The royal ordinance (1463) assigned to the consuls maritime cases arising in Montpelier, Argues-Mortes, Agde and the surrounding district and gave them power " de cognoistre des debats, tout ainsi et en la meme forme et maniere que font et ont accoutumé de faire au consulat de mer de la ville de Perpignan." In the course of a century sea consulates were established at Toulouse (1549), Paris (1563) and Marseilles (1565). It would seem that while the sea consulate as a maritime court first arose in Pisa, the diffusion of the institution throughout Southern and Western Europe was due to its general establishment in Aragon and

---

[1] Pardessus, IV. pp. 231, 232, 235.

to the territorial acquisitions and losses of the
Aragonese royal house in Southern Europe.

Long before the introduction of the sea consulate,
by imitation of the Spanish consulate at Perpignan,
commercial courts existed in France[1]. At Marseilles
consuls and judges of appeal for commercial cases
were elected as early as 1162 and their functions
were solely judicial. The consuls at Narbonne, on
the other hand, though elective and possessed of
judicial powers, can hardly be called commercial
judges in the strict sense of the term, as in addition
to important administrative duties they had jurisdiction in criminal and civil as well as purely
commercial cases. They occupied, in fact, much the
same position as did the Italian town consuls before
the rise of the consules mercatorum as commercial
judges. By some writers the "parloir aux bourgeois[2]"
has been regarded as a commercial court, but its
claim to that title is doubtful. It was the court
of the "Marchands de l'eau" of Paris. To this gild
of merchants Philip Augustus had granted rights of
sovereignty over the course of the Seine. Territorial rights and rights of jurisdiction were inseparable
during the early Middle Ages, and the grant implied
both the power to make regulations for the trade
and navigation of the river, and the power to enforce
those regulations and punish their infraction. To
this duty the "parloir" in the main confined itself,
and of the numerous decisions of the court which
have been preserved the great majority refer to

[1] Morel, *Les Juridictions Commerciales au Moyen Age*, 135—7.
[2] *Op. cit.*, 144—7.

breaches of the privileges of the gild, and it is but very rarely that it determines commercial disputes between individual merchants. It was, as Morel has remarked, only incidentally a commercial court, and its sole importance lies in the fact that as a court composed of judges who were merchants and elected by merchants it may have prepared the way for the creation in the 16th century of the consular judges of Paris, the prototypes of the commercial judges of France from the 16th century to the present time.

Among the commercial tribunals of France the courts of the great fairs of Champagne[1] were until the 15th century the most important. The earliest evidence for the existence of "custodes nundinarum" at these fairs dates from the year 1174. The method of appointment of the guardians of the fair "before the reunion of Champagne and Brie with the French crown is doubtful, but at the commencement of the 14th century they were appointed by the great council of the realm." Originally there were three of these judges, but later the number was reduced to two and finally (1360), as the fairs declined in importance, to one. Though as judges in the greatest fairs of Europe they were mainly occupied in deciding commercial cases, their powers of jurisdiction were not of a purely commercial order. For while on the one hand they had only jurisdiction over merchants and persons frequenting the fairs, and those who wronged merchants on their

---

[1] Morel, *Les Juridictions Commerciales au Moyen Age*, pp. 148—166. Huvelin, *Droit des Marchés*, 244—258, 390—396, 474—479 etc. Bourquelot, *Études sur les Foires de Champagne*.

way to and from the fairs, on the other hand they possessed so far as these persons were concerned a criminal and unlimited civil jurisdiction. The procedure was summary, and appeal lay in the first instance to the "Grands Jours" of Troyes and finally to the Parliament of Paris. By the close of the Middle Ages the Champagne fair, and consequently the fair courts, had lost all importance and during the course of the 17th century it finally disappeared. At Lyons[1] the fair court developed into a permanent court of commerce. Already in existence in the 14th century the Lyons fair was in 1436 placed for judicial purposes under the authority of the royal seneschal of Lyons, who, as conservator of the fair, "had power, authority and commission to judge and determine without long process or figure of pleading all the disputes which might arise between our said officials and the merchants frequenting the fairs in time of fairs." As in Champagne the nomination of the judge was in the hands of the central authority. Twenty years later the office of "conservator" of the fair was separated from that of seneschal, but the nomination still remained in the hands of the king, and it was not till 1655 after many attempts that the consulate of the town obtained a share in the nomination of the judges of the "conservation." The number of judges was in that year fixed by royal ordinance at eleven: the provost of the merchants and the four echevins were members of the tribunal ex officio; of the remaining six judges two were nominated by the king, four by the consulate

[1] Morel, 166—186. Huvelin, *Droit des Marchés*.

from among the merchants or ex-consuls. During the 16th century the Lyons court ceased to be merely a fair court, and a royal letter of 1602 recognises the jurisdiction of the court "tant en foires que hors foires." The attempts of the merchants of Lyons during the 16th century to secure the creation of elective merchant judges is a characteristic feature of the later development of commercial events in France[1]. Such judges were created by royal ordinance in 1549 at Toulouse and in 1563 at Paris. The Parisian judges had jurisdiction in "tous procès ou différens mûs entre marchands pour fait de marchandise seulement" and were elected in indirect fashion by the merchants. Within a year elective merchant judges were established at Nantes, Bordeaux, Poitiers and Tours. The institution became general and, though modified in points of detail, remains in its broad features unchanged in Modern France.

In Germany[2] commercial courts rose later than in Italy or France. The chief cause of the rise of courts solely for commercial cases was the need of a prompt justice that the civil law of France and Italy, which was based mainly upon Roman Law, did not provide. In Germany however, before the reception of Roman Law, the proceedings were mainly oral and offered little opportunity for long delays[3]. It is probably for this reason that in the inland towns of

<hr />

[1] Morel, 188—205.

[2] Silberschmidt, *Die Entstehung des deutschen Handelgerichts*, and Morel.

[3] *Op. cit.*, p. 160.

Germany no special commercial courts arose during the Middle Ages. But the general reception in Germany of the Roman Law during the course of the 14th and 15th centuries made justice less prompt, and the merchants began to demand the creation of special courts. The 15th century saw the rise of maritime courts in the chief towns of the Baltic. At Frankfort the merchants began voluntarily to take their disputes to a court of arbitration which had all the characteristics of a commercial court of justice. There was a definite summary procedure and in cases of doubt the arbitrators consulted previous decisions which were carefully recorded and regarded as authoritative in commercial matters[1]. At Regensburg the merchants seem to have adopted another expedient to avoid the delays to which the Roman process gave rise. During the Middle Ages the German merchants in their journeys from city to city were governed and judged by a hanse-reeve. There is evidence that the Regensburg merchants possessed such officials as early as the 12th century. Their name suggests that they were similar to the Italian gild consuls, but there is a great difference between the two. There is no evidence to show that the hanse-reeve was, like the Italian consul, as a general rule elected by the merchants[2], and he had no powers of jurisdiction within his native city[3].

[1] Morel, 107—8.

[2] Morel, 121.

[3] Keutgen, *Urkunden*, p. 198.   Regensburg Stadtrecht, c. 12 (A.D. 1230). "Item cives potestatem habebunt elegendi hausgravium qui disponat et ordinet extra civitatem et non infra ea tantum que respiciunt negotia nundinarum," cf. Morel, 108.

During the 15th century however the Regensburg hanse-reeve began to exercise jurisdiction in commercial cases within the bounds of the city itself. Repeatedly the schultheiss of the town complains that the inhabitants declare that disputes are of a mercantile character "in order that they may be judged before the hanse court." Von Freyberg includes the court of the hanse-reeve among the Regensburg tribunals and states that it had jurisdiction in commercial cases, of which he especially mentions partnership[1]. As the hanse-reeve was in Regensburg an elective official, his court was of the same pattern as the consular courts of Italy or Marseilles. It was not, however, till the commencement of the 16th century that a commercial court of this type was recognised by the Emperor. In a charter granted to the town of Nuremberg[2] in 1508 the Emperor declared that merchants were the persons best fitted to decide mercantile disputes, and authorised the creation of a number of merchant judges.

The Nuremberg charter however seems, so far as the appointment of merchant judges was concerned, to have been observed for only a short time. But in the following century a commercial court was established (1682) at Leipzig in which the judges were partly laymen and partly jurists, and which served as a model for the later courts of Germany. As in France, the tendency was in favour of lay judges, and in both Germany and France the com-

1 Morel, 109.
2 Silberschmidt, 59.

mercial courts have retained in their main features the form and constitution that they assumed during the 15th and 16th centuries. The commercial judges of modern France are still merchants elected for the purpose, and the modern commercial courts of Germany consist, as did the Leipzig court of 1682, of merchants and of jurists. Italy alone of the three countries has broken completely with the traditions of the past. During the Middle Ages the Italian commercial judges were merchants who sometimes had jurists associated with them; from the close of the Middle Ages down to the 19th century the system of commercial courts composed not of merchants alone, but of merchants and jurists together, gradually became the rule and was but the natural development of the Italian medieval courts. But the recent abolition in Italy of separate commercial courts and the transfer of their jurisdiction to the ordinary courts of common law mark a new departure in the history of the commercial jurisprudence of Italy.

In England as on the continent there were during the Middle Ages numerous local maritime and fair courts; and, when for financial purposes the bulk of the foreign trade of the country was in the 14th century compelled to pass through a few important towns, special courts were created in these staple towns to administer the Law Merchant. A mayor and two constables were chosen annually to hold the court of the staple, which had jurisdiction in all pleas concerning debts, covenant and trespass. As with the judges were associated two merchants chosen respectively from among the merchants who came from the North and those who came from the South, the court evidently constituted a lay tribunal similar to the maritime courts of Spain and the later commercial courts of France.

Appeals lay from the staple courts to the Chancellor and Council, just as in the contemporary fair courts of Champagne appeal could be made to the Parliament of Paris. It would seem that the association of merchants with the commercial judges was in England a recognised institution during the Middle Ages. In the maritime court of Padstow a case reported for the year 1383 shows that the trial took place before the mayor and burgesses assisted by a jury of mariners and merchants[1]. In fair courts the merchants declared the law. The records of St Ives Fair (1275) refer to one of the decisions as "the judgment of the court and of the merchants"; and a few years later in the same court a case is respited "until it shall be more thoroughly discussed by the merchants[2]." The evidence of the 14th century Bristol treatise on this point is most explicit. "In every 'curia mercati,'" it declares, "all judgments are to be given by the merchants of that court and not by the mayor or seneschal. If the mayor or seneschal should presume to give the judgments, the person aggrieved should have remedy

---

[1] Marsden, *Select Pleas of Admiralty*, vol. I. Introduction p. 49.

[2] Maitland, *Select Pleas in Manorial Courts*, p. 137 (1291 A.D.) and p. 147 (1275 A.D.); *v.* Appendix Nos. 1 and 3.

against them as 'contrary to law and custom and
the Law Merchant[1].' "

Fair and Market and Staple courts were all
local courts, but during the 14th century the expansion of English trade and the necessity of checking
piracy led to the creation of royal maritime courts
under the authority of the Admirals of the Fleet.
The earliest instance in England of the use of the title
of admiral dates from the year 1300 when Gervase
Abelard is mentioned as admiral of the fleet of the
Cinque ports, but for half a century there is no
evidence that an admiral's court existed with judicial
powers over non-members of the fleet. In 1357
however there is a reference to a judicial decision of
the admiral in a prize case ; and three years later a
captain of the fleet is appointed with full judicial
powers "querelas omnium et singulorum armatae
praedictae audiendi et delinquentes incarcerandi
castigandi et puniendi et plenam justitiam ac omnia
alia et singula quae ad huiusmodi capitaneum et
ductorem pertinent et pro bono regimine hominum
praedictorum necessaria fuerint faciendi prout de jure
et secundum legem maritimam fuerit faciendum[2]."
A few months later, upon the appointment of a single

---

[1] Chapter 12, p. 70 in *Little Red Book of Bristol*. The "suitors"
of the commercial courts are according to the treatise, c. 12
(p. 71) : " omnes illi qui feoffati sunt et residentes infra limites
civitatum, feriarum, portuum, burgorum et villarum mercatoriarum, et eciam omnes mercatores qui *ex consuetudine* ferias illas
seu mercata visitant, et illi quorum nomina in papiro sunt mercati
nisi sint clerici vel clericali statu utentes, Comites, Barones,
Baroneti, vel milites."

[2] Marsden, *S. Pleas of Admiralty*, Introduction, p. 42.

admiral to command the whole English fleet, a royal
patent was issued authorising the admiral to appoint
a deputy and "giving to him full power...of hearing
plaints of all and singular the matters that touch
the office of the admiral and of taking cognisance
of maritime causes and of doing justice and of
correcting and punishing offences and of imprisoning
and of setting at liberty prisoners who ought to
be set at liberty, and of doing all other things that
appertain to the office of admiral as they ought to
be done of right and according to the law maritime[1].
The jurisdiction of the Court of Admiralty as
established by the admiral's patent was vague and
gave the court full scope to extend its power.
Complaints were made by the local courts of the
encroachments of the Court upon their jurisdiction.
"Because," declares a statute[2] of 1390, "great and
common clamour and plaint have often been made
before this time and still are made that the admirals
and their deputies hold their sessions in divers
places within the realm, both within franchise and
without, taking to themselves greater power than
belongs to their office, to the prejudice of our Lord
the king and of the common law of the realm and to
the great damage of divers franchises, it is granted
that the admirals and their deputies shall not in
future meddle with anything done within the
kingdom, but only with anything done upon the sea
as was the custom in the time of the noble King
Edward III." This act does not seem to have been

---

[1] Marsden, S. *Pleas of Admiralty*, Introduction, p. 43.
[2] *Black Book of Admiralty*, I. 412.

found sufficient to restrain the encroachments of the admiralty, for two years later the limits of its jurisdiction were more carefully defined. "It is declared, ordained and determined," runs the statute, " that of all contracts pleas and plaints and of all other things done and arising within the body of counties as well by water as by land and also of wreck of the sea, the court of the admiral shall have no cognisance, power or jurisdiction; but that all such contracts, pleas and plaints and all other things rising within the bodies of counties as well by land as by sea as aforesaid and also wreck of the sea shall be tried, determined and discussed and remedied by the laws of the land and not before the admiral nor his lieutenant in any way : nevertheless of the death of a man and of a mayhem done in great ships being and hovering in the main stream of great rivers, only beneath the bridges of the same rivers near the sea and in no other places of the same rivers the admiral shall have cognisance[1]." Shortly after the accession of Henry IV. a remedy was provided for those who had been sued, contrary to the terms of the statute of Richard II., in the Court of Admiralty, enabling them to recover double damages in the ordinary courts from the plaintiff, who was moreover liable to a fine of £10. The common law courts issued frequent writs of prohibition based upon the statute of 1392 and checked encroachments on the part of the admiral's jurisdiction. At first the admiralty adopted the system of trial by jury, which was still in vogue

---

[1] *Black Book of Admiralty*, I. 413, 414.

in the middle of the 15th century[1]. By the middle
of the 16th century however the jury system had
been replaced by trial by witnesses. The procedure
and the law administered were largely based upon
the Roman civil law. The towns of Bristol, Bridg-
water, Exeter, Barnstaple and Wells complain as
early as the reign of Richard II. "of the delays of
the law civil," and in the 15th century "articles of
the lieutenant general of the high admiral" it was
provided that the judges " should only mix the law
civil with the law maritime there where it may
be equitable." The activity of the court increased
under the Tudors, but during the 17th century a
determined attack was made upon its jurisdiction
by the common law courts. The attack was in the
main successful, and most of the civil jurisdiction
of the Admiralty courts was usurped by the courts
of common law, and not recovered till the 19th
century.

It was not only at the expense of the Admiralty
that the common law courts extended their jurisdiction. During the 15th century the merchant
gilds in England lost much of their importance ;
and though a few fair courts still continued and the
courts of some of the larger cities retained their
jurisdiction, the common law courts began to occupy
themselves with commercial cases of every kind.
During the 17th century the decisions of Lord Holt
and Lord Mansfield introduced into English common
law most of the customs and usages of English

[1] Marsden, *S. P. of A.*, Introduction, 54. *Black Book of
Admiralty*, vol. I. p. 267.

merchants, and the Law Merchant became an integral part of the common law of the realm, and the common law courts practically the only courts where commercial cases were decided. While France and Germany still adhere to the medieval system of separate commercial courts entirely or partly composed of lay judges, England had by the 17th century already begun to transfer the jurisdiction over commercial cases to the ordinary law courts, and by the 18th century the process was practically complete. But to the local commercial courts of the Middle Ages and to their merchant judges Western Europe owes a great debt. Out of their own needs the medieval merchants created their own courts and in those courts evolved, expanded and systematized a body of commercial law, speedy, equitable and flexible, which forms the basis of the commercial rules of modern times.

CHAPTER IV.

PERSONS.

THE merchant was during the two or three centuries that followed the rise of the Law Merchant almost invariably a member of a gild which early acquired a monopoly of trade for its members. In England such clauses as " We grant a gild merchant with a hanse and other customs belonging to the gild so that no one who is not of the gild may merchandise in the said town except with the consent of the burgesses " are found in practically all the Merchant gild charters from the 13th century onward. Though in most of the countries of the continent the gild did not exercise the influence upon the government of the town that it often exercised in England, nearly everywhere the gild existed and secured for its members, in early times at any rate, a practical monopoly of trade. It would be wrong indeed to assert that even during the early period of the gild system all who were actually engaged in trade belonged without exception to a gild, but for long such cases were the exception and not the rule. The general insecurity and lawlessness that characterised the early centuries of the Middle Ages forced the medieval merchant to organise and to combine in order to defend his own interests. But though the gild was perhaps at first a necessary expedient in a lawless age, it proved, with its tendency towards exclusiveness and its narrow-minded desire to develop not so much the trade of the whole country as the trade of its own locality, a hindrance rather than a help to the development of commerce as order was gradually established and nations and kingdoms gradually rose out of feudal anarchy. When towards the close of the Middle Ages France and Spain, Sicily and England, Denmark and Scandinavia formed well organised kingdoms, a commercial system that regarded the merchant of one city as an alien when trading in another city of the same kingdom no longer corresponded to the needs of the time. Commerce had outgrown the period of municipal exclusiveness that the gild system represented, and the gild everywhere lost much of its power and importance. Gradually the merchant was freed from the necessity of joining the gild and the development of commerce was left to individual initiative and enterprise. The gild however proved to be long lived, and centuries after it had outlived its day of usefulness it continued in some countries to enforce rules and regulations no longer adapted to the new political and economic conditions of Europe.

In Italy the emancipation of the individual merchant from the monopoly of the gild began early; for in commercial development it was far in advance of other countries and it realised earlier than was realised in most countries the evils of absolutely confining trade and commerce to a close corporation. As elsewhere, the privilege of trading and manufacturing was at first confined, with rare exceptions, to members of the various gilds, and the old rule was maintained in many places until the close of the Middle Ages and even later[1]. As early as the 13th century however some of the town statutes freed both merchant and citizen from the obligation of entering a gild; and the frequent employment in the statutes of such expressions as "consueti," "usitati," "usevoli mercatores" shows that in Italy there existed during the 14th and 15th centuries a well recognised class of merchants who were not members of the gild[2]. The same change, though generally later than in Italy, took place elsewhere, and slowly it became no longer necessary for the trader to be a member of a gild to enjoy the legal privileges of a merchant. Foremost among those privileges was the right to be judged by the Law Merchant. That law was in its origin a personal law, the law of a special class. In virtue of his profession the merchant had a right to be judged by a law different from the common law. It was a law based largely upon the usages and customs of the merchant class and often administered by the merchants themselves. The Law Merchant in the main retained throughout the Middle Ages this characteristic feature. In England the view that

[1] Lattes, p. 82, note 1. Pertile, vol. II. part i. p. 180.
[2] Lattes, p. 81 and notes.

the application of the principles of the Law Merchant
was a legal privilege, to which the merchant alone
could lay claim, was maintained in part till the end
of the 17th century. In 1613 the plea that an
acceptor of a bill of exchange was not a merchant
was held by the court to be a good defence to a
claim on the bill, and it was not till 1692 that the
English courts ventured to ignore the personal
character of the Law Merchant by deciding that if
gentlemen accepted bills they ought to pay them[1].
France had effected the same development a century
earlier, and the Paris court of commerce, which was
established in 1563, and the numerous courts of
which it was the model, had jurisdiction and applied
the Law Merchant in all cases of bills of exchange
whether the parties to the suit were merchants or
not. The main course in the development of the
legal status of the merchant would seem to be that
this status, long confined to members of a close
corporation, was gradually extended to all those
actually engaged in trade, and that the merchant
gradually ceased to have an exclusive claim to
the speedy and practical justice of the Law
Merchant.

In countries where the Roman Law prevailed
the Law Merchant does not seem in early times to
have been able to secure freedom of contract for the
married woman. In Italy, for example, she could
only carry on business with the consent, express or
tacit, of her husband, who was responsible in virtue
of that consent for the execution of all contracts

[1] Sarsfield v. Witherby, Carthew 82, quoted by Scrutton, p. 30.

that she might make[1]. In the case of "filii familias," however, the influence of German law and the necessities of commerce triumphed over the maxims of Roman law even in Italy, where the common law of the land was in the main Roman, and a filius familias actually engaged in trade on his own account was considered "sui juris" even though he continued to live in his father's house[2].

The agents and factors of the merchant were in Italy subject like the merchant himself to the jurisdiction of the commercial courts and they could claim to be judged according to the Law Merchant in commercial disputes with one another or with their master. In case of their employer's failure they were in many Italian towns held liable, under certain circumstances, for his debts, and they had the right to conclude contracts binding upon the merchant whose factor they were[3]. Consequently the distinction between factor and partner was often of no great practical importance; and in a letter sent from Pisa to Florence in 1310 it was declared that in mercantile usage "factor" and "socius" had the same significance[4].

In England however as late as the reign of Edward I. the whole common "law of agency was still in its infancy." But whatever view the king's courts might take, the Law Merchant in England recognised in the 13th century that when an agent

[1] Pertile, III. pp. 309, 310.
[2] Pertile, vol. III. p. 380, n. 32.
[3] Lattes, p. 103, notes 11 and 14. Goldschmidt, pp. 249, 250.
[4] Goldschmidt, 250, n. 51.

bought goods the property was vested in the principal not in the agent. A case in the fair court of St Ives for the year 1291 illustrates this point. Hugo Pope was distrained in a suit by means of a horse. "And thereupon a certain Alan of Berkhamstead comes—and alleged in full court that the said horse was his and that he had bought the horse for his own for use of a certain Thomas of 'Rammesden,' and he placed himself of his own free will on the inquest, and the opposite party likewise. And the inquest—comes and says that the said Alan unjustly claims the horse as his own; nor has he any part in the horse because the said Alan bought the horse to the use of the aforesaid Hugo as the 'valet' and broker of Hugo; and Hugo instructed him to pay 20 shillings in the name of Hugo for the horse—wherefore it was considered that the horse be kept and taken until the aforesaid Hugo shall have given satisfaction[1]."

The Bristol Treatise on the Lex Mercatoria gives a valuable account of the legal relations of master and servant in their bearing upon transactions with third parties. "Because frequently and generally it happens," the treatise declares, "that apprentices and 'sub-merchants' who publicly and openly trade under their masters procure the loan and accommodation of money, goods and merchandise to their masters' use, and if they were borrowing by themselves and not for masters of this kind, one would not deliver to them goods at all,—it is ordained that the masters of these apprentices and sub-merchants shall in the same way be answerable

[1] See Appendix No. 4.

for goods and merchandise delivered to them in any way by the hands of their apprentices and sub-merchants just as if they themselves had received those goods and merchandise with their own hands, provided that the apprentices and agents (submercatores) are known to be under their master and to be openly serving and trading with the goods of their master before and after an exchange or delivery of this kind, or at any rate at the time of such exchange and delivery. Moreover if their property has been advanced, handed over or in any way delivered by their agents or other of their men, the merchants have the same action against all persons in suing for their goods and merchandise as if they themselves had advanced, delivered or handed over the goods and merchandise[1]." The Law Merchant in England recognised the responsibility of the principal for the acts of his agent provided that the agency was open and well known, and based that responsibility upon the equitable grounds that credit was generally given to the agent simply because it was believed that he was acting on behalf of his master.

If the merchant enjoyed many privileges in his own country and elsewhere, as a foreigner he was subject when abroad to many legal disabilities, which were partly a survival from primitive times when the stranger in a foreign land was a rightless person unprotected by the law. Defenceless as he was the foreign merchant in olden times obtained a security that the law did not give by placing himself under

[1] Chapter VII. *Little Red Book of Bristol*, p. 66.

the protection of a powerful individual able and willing to protect him. It was even in historical times often a very necessary precaution. "The Saxons sold the stranger who had no patron[1]." Gradually the head of the State took the foreign merchant under his special protection, but the stranger had to pay the price. Not only was he often subject to dues and tolls that the native merchants did not pay, but if he died intestate and without children the king, and where feudalism triumphed the local authorities, laid claim to any of his property that happened to be within their jurisdiction. It would seem that during the 12th and 13th centuries this right of "aubaine" became more oppressive. Originally the stranger had a right to make a will, and if he had children they succeeded to his possessions, but the feudal lord and the free commune, and in France the king himself, overrode both testament and rights of the stranger's children[2].

It is to the credit of the Papacy and the Church that it used its vast influence to remedy this injustice; and as early as the middle of the 12th century (1109) the Pope abolished the "jus Albanagii" within the papal States. The influence of the Church was not exerted in vain, and Frederick II. (1220) forbade the exercise of the right within the bounds of his Empire[3].

[1] Meginardi, *Translat. S. Vitti*, c. 13, "Peregrinum qui patronem non habebat vendebant Saxones." Quoted by Pertile, III. 187, n. 1.

[2] Pertile, III. 194. Viollet, *Histoire de Droit...*p. 368. For the right of aubaine in general see Caillemer, *Confiscation et administration des successions*, 147, 178.

[3] Schroeder, *Deutsche Rechtsgeschichte*, p. 530; note 52.

But the decline of the imperial power in Italy led in that country to a revival of the custom, while in France the financial necessities of the crown increased the severity of the law. Not only were the children of the alien debarred from their father's inheritance, but a new maxim—"aubains ne peuvent succéder" —was added to the old adage "aubains ne peuvent tester." But the custom ran counter to the true interests of commerce. The law itself the merchant was unable during the Middle Ages to abolish, but the great mercantile cities and countries by special treaties procured exemption from the law for their citizens, the richer merchants effected the same purposes by obtaining letters of naturalisation, and the greater fairs were gradually freed, in France if not elsewhere, from the operation of the law. In 1364, for example, all the Castilian merchants trading in France were exempted from the right of aubaine; and in 1340 a merchant in return for hard cash obtained recognition of the right of his children to inherit, and of his own right of testation "tout aussi bien comme sil fust nez franchement de nostre royaume; et voulons que pour cette cause il ne doie, ne puisse jamais estre reputez pour aubaine, epave, ou etrange de nostre royaume." As early as 1294 a treaty concluded between the captain of the Lombards frequenting the fairs of Champagne, and the Count of Salins, established that " if any of these merchants die within our land or jurisdiction, or their messenger or servant, we will cause his goods to be consigned and rendered to his messenger or partner—or to the messenger of the union of the said merchants or of the captain, as soon as they have been demanded from us or our bailiff; but he who has received the goods shall carry the will of the deceased." The privilege was extended to a great number of fairs[1]. A 15th century ordinance (1465) of the fair of Chalon-sur-Saône granted permission " to all the said foreign merchants to make wills and provide for the disposal of their property according to their good pleasure. And in case the said foreign merchants should die in our land intestate, those who ought to inherit according to the written law, the statutes or customs of the country, inherit fully and without opposition, as if they had died in the place of their nativity or where they abode." But in spite of numerous exemptions the old disability still continued to be recognised by the law and was not abolished in Savoy till 1633 and in France till the French Revolution[2].

The exercise of the right of aubaine was greatly limited during the course of the Middle Ages by the rise of national kingdoms and the increase of the power of the crown throughout the greater part of Europe. The feudal lord had been inclined to regard the mere stranger to the locality as subject to the right of aubaine even though he might be a citizen of the country, while the king only exercised the right over strangers to the realm.

The aliens however were subject to restrictions of a more purely commercial character than was the right of aubaine. The usage of commercial towns

---

[1] Huvelin, *Droit des Marchés*, pp. 444, 445.
[2] Pertile, III. pp. 197, 198 and notes 47 and 54.

in medieval Europe confined the trade of foreign
merchants within the narrowest limits. As a
general rule they were not allowed, except in fairs
and in some towns on certain market days, to buy
from or sell to other strangers, and retail trade was
very often absolutely forbidden. During their stay
they were to lodge with a "host" appointed by the
town or gild magistrates, and the host was held
responsible for the behaviour of his guests and
expected to see that they did not infringe the rights
of the citizen by retail trade or by dealing with other
strangers. On the whole these restrictions were
maintained till the end of the Middle Ages. In
England indeed the foreign merchant, to the great
discontent of the towns, was freed during great part
of the reigns of Edward III. and Richard II. from
these restrictions, but under the Lancastrian kings
they were once more reimposed. The rule that the
foreign merchant should "go to host" seems in
England to have fallen into disuse in the 15th
century, but that it was maintained on the continent
is shown by the bitter complaint of a pamphleteer
that the foreigner fared better in England than the
English abroad.

> "What reason is't that we should go to host
> In their countries, and in this English Coast
> They should not so; but have more liberty
> Than we ourselves[1]."

To this desire to limit and control the operations
of foreign merchants in the interests of the locality

---

[1] Quoted in Ashley, *Economic History*, vol. i. part ii. p. 17.

is partly due the important position that the brokers[1] gradually acquired. In the Roman Empire brokers already existed but, unorganised and un-controlled by the laws, they occupied a far less important position than fell to their lot during the Middle Ages. Ulpian calls their occupation sordid, and Horace describes the merchant who had failed to succeed when trading on his own account as a last resource turning broker. In the Middle Ages how-ever brokers had almost attained on the continent to the rank of public officials. They were as a rule limited in number, appointed by the gild or city magistrates, and required to be of good repute and citizens of the town. At times the regulations plainly show that the brokers were appointed in the interests of the local monopoly. "We appoint," declares a decree[2] of the town council of Vienna of the year 1348, "for the merchant and traders six brokers who are landowners, and true and honest folk who shall go into their bargains, and they and no one else shall truly serve strangers and citizens ......and every broker, when he learns that a stranger is travelling through the land against the right of the town and the gild, shall bring the matter before

[1] For the position of brokers in Medieval Italy see Rezzara, *Dei Mediatori e del Contratto di Mediazione*, in which numerous and long quotations are given from various city statutes of Italy.

[2] Keutgen, *Urkunden*, No. 236, p. 330. St. Calimalae (Florence 1301), Lb. v. cap. 1, p. 157, "Item jurent *sensales denumptiare secrete consulibus* Kallismale omnes et singulos mercatores facien-tes contra formam capituli constituti hujus vel contra ordi-namenta loquentia de sicuritate averis Kallismale et hominum dicte artis et de *retinentibus hospitum forensium et de scribentibus et promictentibus pro forensibus et de ipsis forensibus......*"

the gild reeve as he has sworn to do." It was
everywhere their duty to keep a written account of
the transactions which had been arranged by their
mediation. At Cologne[1] (c. 1400) "to avoid all
quarrels and disputes which might arise between
merchants with regard to money or sales, the hosts
and brokers were to swear to write down every sale."
In the Italian statutes the duties and legal privileges
are treated with unusual detail, and their position as
public officials is recognised by the law courts. In
disputed cases the courts admitted the principle that
the evidence of the broker's books was to be regarded
as correct unless there was definite proof of the
contrary.

The 13th century gild statutes of Piacenza
declare "that if a dispute arise about contracts or the
price of goods, the broker who arranged the bargain
shall be believed on his simple word," while the
statutes of Cremona[2] (1388) which contain a similar
regulation show with what care the books were
required to be kept. "The brokers are bound to
write with their own hand, or to have written, all the
sales which they make of the value of 25 imperial
pounds or above, if complete payment has not been
made, in a book, which shall be kept at the office of
the gild with the consuls and shall be bought with
the money of the gild, declaring the name and sur-
name of the buyer and seller, the article sold and
its price and the date fixed for payment; and this
they are bound to do within eight days of the day

[1] Keutgen, *Urkunden*, No. 237, cap. 12, p. 331.
[2] Quoted by Rezzara in *Dei Mediatori*, p. 53.

that the bargain was made......and the book placed
in the office of the gild shall be believed unless
there is proof to the contrary." To secure impartiality it was a general rule that no merchant or
partner of a merchant should be a broker, and that
if he had a personal interest in any transaction he
should inform the parties. Occasionally the statutes
go further and absolutely forbid the broker to
negotiate the sale of any goods in which he is in
any way interested. Appointed as he was by the
authorities, authorised to report the misdeeds of
foreigners and to keep a record of their sales and
contracts, in which his mediation was often declared
necessary by the laws, and possessed of a legal claim
to be believed in virtue of his office[1], the medieval
broker occupied on the continent a position of public
trust and authority which he did not possess in the
Roman Empire and which he no longer retains in
modern times.

[1] St. of Bergamo 14, cap. 57. "Mesetti (*i.e.* brokers) teneantur
in scriptis dare quodlibet mercatum...et tali mercato in scriptis
producto credatur et plena fides adhibeatur." St. of Brescia,
cap. 9, same expressions verbatim.

CHAPTER V.

SALES AND CONTRACTS.

IN sales neither Roman nor Germanic law satisfied the requirements of the medieval merchant, and
very early traders began to assert maxims of their
own better suited to their needs. It was in market
and fair that in all probability the new rules first
became customs that ripened into laws. Early in
the 11th century a German poet writes that merchants were asserting the validity of sales made in
fairs, though concluded without the usual formalities.
That the merchants should try to alter the existing
law regulating sale and possession of goods is not
surprising. Neither Roman nor Germanic law gave
to the bargains of merchants that security and
certainty that the interests of commerce demanded.
Neither protected against the claims of the original
owner the merchant who had in perfect good faith
bought goods stolen or lost, and neither secured the
validity of a sale confirmed by an earnest. According
to Roman law the rights of the original owner
remained good against all third parties whether they
had acquired possession in good faith or not, and

whether the goods had been stolen from the owner himself or from a person to whom he had entrusted them.

The laws of the Teutonic nations, however, only recognised the right of the original owner of stolen property to make good his claim against third parties, if it was actually in his own possession when it had been lost or stolen. If he had lent or entrusted the article to any one from whom it was afterwards stolen, he had only a right of action against the person to whom it had been confided[1].

But this did not make the position of the bona fide purchaser more secure; for though the original owner had lost all right of action against third parties, that right had merely passed to the person to whom the goods had been entrusted. A merchant was at any time liable to be called upon to defend his right to goods that he had purchased, if they should prove to be stolen or lost property. If he could not name the person from whom he had bought them, he not only lost his property but ran the risk

---

[1] Schroeder, p. 273.

Pertile, IV. 256 and notes 26 and 27.

Sachsenspiegel II. 61, § 1. "Welcher Mann...fahrende Habe dem anderen leiht oder versetzt, verkauft sie dieser, wird sie ihm gestohlen oder geraubt; jener mag darum keine Foderung haben, als gegen den dem er sie lieh oder versetzte."

Brunner, *Rechtsgeschichte*, II. 509. "Wurde die Sache nicht dem Eigentümer, sondern einer treuen Hand gestohlen, in der er sie gelegt hatte, so war nur diese in der Lage, den 'Anefang' durchzuführen und die Diebstahlsbusse in Anspruch zu nehmen."

Friese und Liesegang, *Magdeburger Schöffensprüche*, Nos. 1, 1. III. A 45, pp. 4, 418, 709, 710.

Maitland, *History of E. L.* II. 163—6.

of being punished as a thief. Even if he was in a position to produce the seller, he did not retain the goods, and the vouchee whom he had produced was called upon to explain how the goods had come into his possession. He could defend himself in the same way by producing as warrant the person from whom he had made the purchase, and it would seem that the process could at first be continued indefinitely. Gradually, however, the process came almost everywhere to be regarded as complete when the third warrant appeared before the Court[1].

That in the 13th century English merchants were attempting to secure protection in the possession of stolen goods bought in market and fair, and that their claim was not recognised by the king's courts, is apparent from the evidence of the legal writers of the time. "If the accused," writes Britton[2], "has any warrant within our realm, then he may defend himself by voucher, and if he vouched to warrant any person who gave him the thing, or sold it or otherwise made it over to him, let a day be given him to produce his warrant if he be not present.......If the vouchee comes and enters into the warranty to defend the voucher in the possession of the thing, let the plea against the principal be suspended and one commenced against the warrant. And if the warrant

---

[1] Brunner II. 503 and notes 51—5. Brunner quotes Otto I.'s legislation, "Tunc tercius warens juret quod nec latro fuit, nec collega latronis, sed cum suo proprio pretio comparavit et *reddat rem*," and refers to Canute II. 24 § 2, William I. 45, Leges Henrici primi c. 64, § 6. Cf. Pertile IV. 252 note 13; cf. however case (c. 1500) cited above, p. 94, note, *Magdeburger Schöffensprüche*, III A 45.

[2] Britton, edited by Nichols, I. 57—60.

makes good his case then let both the voucher and his warrant be acquitted and the plaintiff sent to prison.......If the judgment be given against the warrant, then the thing challenged shall be adjudged to the plaintiff and the principal shall be indicted of felony at our suit, upon presumption of his being an accomplice of the warrant who is attainted of the felony. If the principal has no one to vouch, he may say that he bought the thing at such a fair or such a market in the presence of a great number of people, and paid a toll to the bailiffs for it. And if he vouches the testimony of the said bailiffs and other then present and evidence is given accordingly, or if he put himself on the country and is acquitted of the felony, and yet the prosecutor has proved that the thing challenged belonged to him and that it was stolen from him or out of his custody, in such case he must be answerable to the owner and give him satisfaction, and judgment shall be that the claimant recover the thing challenged and that the person challenged go quit and lose what he gave for the thing; and if he can produce no such witnesses let him acquit himself by the country." Evidently merchants were beginning to urge that a distinction should be drawn between stolen goods bought in market and fair and those bought elsewhere. The evidence of Bracton is equally strong. " If a person should buy a stolen article, though he believe it to be legally purchasable, then if he cannot produce a warrantor, a distinction must be made whether he has bought it publicly in a fair or in a market, and in the presence of the bailiffs and other honest men who might give testimony of the fact and that he paid toll and customs; such a purchaser shall be set free when he has returned the article to the true owner; but nothing shall be returned to him of the price which he paid; but if he have none of these defences he will be in peril[1]."

As late as the 13th century "stolen goods can be recovered by legal action not only from the hands of the thief, but from the hands of the third, the fourth, the twentieth possessor, even though those hands are clean and there has been a purchase in open market[2]." Evidently the law hampered sale and barter. "Commercial business cannot be carried on if we have to inquire into the title of everybody who comes to us with documents of title such as bills of lading or for the sale of goods[3]."

The financial necessities of the Lords of market and fair, and the increasing importance that was attached partly under the influence of the Church to the element of good faith, contributed to the triumph of the principles asserted by the merchant classes. Fairs and markets were most valuable sources of revenue to the feudal lord, who was not slow in seeing that to protect the honest purchaser in the possession of his goods was likely to increase the importance and consequently the revenue of his fair. Gradually sales in market and fair were specially protected. The merchant who had purchased in good faith was either allowed to keep possession of the goods or at the worst only bound to return

---

[1] Bracton, Fol. 151.   [2] Pollock and Maitland, II. 165.
[3] Scrutton, *Mercantile Law*, p. 23.

them if the original owner was willing to refund the price that had been paid for them. But if the thing shall have been sold, declares the fair charter of Chapelande[1] for the year 1075, and the buyer has lawfully proved that he was unaware that it was a thief from whom he bought it......(the owner) shall have his property and pay the buyer what he gave for it. Beaumanoir writing in the 13th century gives the same rule. "But if he, who has the thing, has bought it in common market, he, who is claiming his property which he has lost or which was stolen from him, shall not have it back, if he does not refund the money which the buyer paid for it[2]." In Italy the statutes of Nice established that anyone who bought anything openly and in good faith "shall not be bound to return it to its owner, unless he restore to the buyer the price which he had paid." By the 14th century the principle that purchase in open market gave sure possession in stolen goods, or entitled the purchaser to claim the price, was gaining ground in France, Germany and Italy[3], and a case

[1] Huvelin, *Droit des Marchés et des Foires*, p. 455.

[2] Beaumanoir, cited by Pertile iv. 258, note 35. "Se chil qui a la chose l'acheta al marchié quemun, chil qui poursuit sa chose—qu'il perdit ou qui li fu emblé, ne la raura pas se il ne rend l'argent que l'acheterres en paia. Mais si il l'avoit achetée hors de marchié par mendre pris que la chose ne vauroit—et il ne pouvoit trouver son garant, li demandierres rauroit la chose sans l'argent de la vente paier."

[3] Pertile, iv. p. 258 and numerous quotations and references in note 35.

Goldschmidt, p. 299 note 3.

Schroeder, *Deutsche Rechtsgeschichte*, p. 711 and note 11.

Heusler, *Deutsches Privatrecht*, ii. p. 215. "Wichtiger ist

tried in the fair court of St Ives for the year 1291 would seem to show that, though not yet adopted by the courts of common law, the principle of bona fide possession had already become part of the Law Merchant in England. A certain Alice complains of Mathilda Frances "about three bushels of malt found in the hands of the said Mathilda." The plaintiff was obliged to find surety that she would prosecute the case. But when the case came before the court she refused to pursue the plea, and she and her pledges were punished and the case was not allowed to drop. "Thereupon," continues the roll, "the seneschal ex officio, as though on the suit of the king, demanded of the said Mathilda Frances in whose seisin the malt has been found, how she wished to defend herself (from the charge) that the malt had not been acquired by theft. And she says that for good and for ill she placed herself on God, and the sworn neighbours; who come and say on their oath that a certain stranger whom Mathilda herself did not know had brought the malt to her house, and that upon the malt Mathilda had given him in exchange eight pence, and that she did not suspect the stranger of any theft. And therefore it is considered that the said Mathilda together with her malt be quit[1]."

die Neuerung zu Gunsten des gutgläubigen Erwerbers. Sie besteht darin dass wer eine gestohlene Sache auf offenem Markte gekauft hat, gegen die Klage des Bestohlenen geschützt wird."

Jobbé-Duval, *Revindication des Meubles*, pp. 148—9 and notes.

Huvelin, *Droit des Marchés et des Foires*, pp. 455—466.

[1] See Appendix, No. v.

As a general rule it was only sales in markets and fairs that during the Middle Ages gave secure possession of stolen goods. The Jews in Germany and Italy were indeed secured in the possession of stolen articles that they had acquired in good faith[1]; it would seem in the Netherlands[2] that bona fide possession was universally protected, and the principle was applied in Hamburg and some other seaport towns[3] to merchandise that came from beyond the seas. But such cases were but exceptions to the common law of the countries of Western Europe. In France and Germany the old Germanic law, that the person from whom goods had been actually stolen had a right of action against third parties, was in the main observed throughout the later centuries of the Middle Ages. "When French and German law take shape in the 13th century, they contain a rule which is sometimes stated by the words 'Mobilia non habent sequelam' ('Les meubles n'ont pas de suite'), or to use a somewhat enigmatical phrase that became current in Germany, 'Hand muss Hand wahren.'......Where I have put my trust, there must I seek it. We have not here to deal with rules which in the interests of Free Trade protect that favourite of modern law, the bona fide purchaser. Neither the positive nor the negative rule pays any heed to good or bad faith. If my goods go from me without my will I can recover

---

[1] Pertile, IV. 258, n. 34. Schroeder, 710 note 9.

[2] Schroeder, 711 and note 12.

[3] Hamburg, Statute of 1270, VII. 9, Breve Pisani communis 1286, Lb. i. rub. 135.

them from the hundredth hand however clean it may be; if they go from me with my will, I have no action against anyone except my bailee[1]." On the other hand in the medieval documents, that mention special rules applicable to sales in market overt, the element of good faith is often expressly recognised[2]. Gradually the privilege was extended in many towns to all the places where commercial transactions were arranged and no longer confined to those concluded in fair or market place[3]. This medieval custom protecting the honest purchaser in open market has passed into the common law of Italy and France, Germany and Austria, and in England a somewhat extended form of the privilege was adopted by the common law. "In the country the market place or piece of ground set apart by custom for the sale of goods is in general the only

---

[1] Pollock and Maitland, *H. E. L.* II. 155.

[2] Huvelin, note 1, p. 462, and note 2, page 463, quotes several examples: among them, Bouteiller, *Somme rural*, "Mais quant à l'usaige coustumier enca la rivière de Somme, s'il est aucun qui ait acheté aucune chose en plein marché *de bonne foi et bien ne congnoisse le vendeur...*"

Coutume de Perpignan. "Item, si quis rem furtivam in nundinis vel in foro vel publice in platea *bona fide* emerit, non cogitur etc...."

Coutume de Vienne. "Non teneatur domino rem suam restituere, etiamsi suam probaverit,...; nisi probaret legitime ipsum emtorem vel creditorem scivisse tempore empcionis rem esse alienam."

Franchise de Genève. "Item si aliquis res mobiles emerit... publice in nundinis, foro et loco publico, infra civitatem, rem furtivam *bona fide et sine fraude.*"

[3] *Franchises de Toulouse,* p. 2. *Rubr. de Empt.* 3. "Quod si aliquis emerit res mobiles in Tolosa publice vel foro, vel in die fori, vel etiam die"; and cf. note 2 above.

market overt there; but in London and in other towns, when so warranted by custom, a sale in an open shop is equivalent to and in fact amounts to a sale in market overt." The rule was developed by the medieval merchant in fair and market, town and seaport, and to him is mainly due the recognition in modern codes of the claims of the bona fide purchaser. He demanded and rightly demanded that in mercantile transactions conducted openly and in the usual resorts of merchants, there should be presumption of good faith. "The practice of merchants," said Lord Bowen, "is not based upon the supposition of possible fraud......Credit, not distrust, is the basis of commercial dealings[1]."

But the idea of good faith, an idea urged by the Church and supported by the merchants, did more than create a rule protecting the honest purchaser in market and fair. Slowly it undermined the Roman and Germanic principle that in general formless contracts are not binding. "The Germanic races not only of the Karlingian period, but down to a much later time, had no general notion whatever of a promise or agreement as a source of civil obligation. Early Germanic law recognised, if we speak in Roman terms, only Formal and Real Contracts. It had not gone so far as to admit a Consensual contract in any case. Sale, for example, was a Real not a Consensual transaction. All recent inquirers seem to concur in accepting this much as having been conclusively

---

[1] Sanders v. McLean, 11, Q.B.D. p. 343. Quoted by Scrutton, *Mercantile Law*, p. 23.

established[1]." In a few cases Roman law enforced the execution of formless agreements, but such cases were exceptional, and the general principle that "nuda pacta" were not obligatory remained an integral part of the system of Roman law. According to the two great systems of law that prevailed in Western Europe a man was not legally bound by a simple promise devoid of legal form. This view the Church strongly opposed, maintaining that a man was bound by his word rather than by the dispositions of the laws, and a great 13th century Canonist writing on pacts declared that according to Canon Law they should be observed in all cases, even though formless, " because between a simple word and an oath God draws no distinction[2]." The canonical view of the inviolability of agreements gained ground. " All agreements," remarked Beaumanoir who wrote in the 13th century, " are to be kept, for as the saying runs, an agreement overrides law." In the same spirit the Assize of Jerusalem declared that " if any man makes any agreement against the assize and proves it, the agreement made and proved must be kept, for the adage is ' convenant vaine lei[3].' " It was but slowly however that the principle was generally recognised by the civil law. In France it only passed in the 15th century into the treatises on civil law in the work of Panormitain, Archbishop of Palermo, who declared outright " that

[1] Pollock and Maitland, *H. E. L.* II. 185.

[2] Hostiensis, ad tit. de pactis, § quid sit effectus. Quoted by Pollock and Maitland, II. 195.

[3] Pertile IV. 450, note 1.

a simple promise or agreement is as valid as the
stipulations of Roman law[1]." In Germany, while
there were attempts here and there from the end of
the 13th century onward to override the old formalism
of the law of contracts, that formal system on the
whole maintained its ground throughout the whole
course of the Middle Ages[2]. In England Canon
and Roman law early lost the power to shape the
development of English law, and "before the end of
Edward I.'s reign the King's court had established
the rule that the only convention that can be enforced
by action is one that is expressed in a written document sealed by the party that is to be charged there-
with[3]." "Of informal executory agreements there
was in general no remedy in the King's courts[4]."

It would seem however that in commercial disputes the principle of good faith received a wider
and earlier application. In Italy it was recognised
by Bartolo and Baldo, the great jurists of the
14th century, that, in acts of commerce, informal
contracts were binding ; and this peculiarity in
mercantile usage they attempted to explain by an
appeal to the principles of equity ; this mercantile
usage was repeatedly recognised by later writers[5].

[1] Viollet, *Histoire du droit civil français*, p. 600.
[2] Schroeder, 730. For reception of principle see p. 787.
Heusler, *Privatrecht*, II. 245 and 227.
[3] Pollock and Maitland, II. 219.
[4] Pollock, *Contracts*, 140.
[5] Pertile, IV. 451 note 5. Goldschmidt, 305, note 33.
Lattes, *Il Diritto Commerciale*, pp. 123 and 129 : notes 1—3
give copious references.
St. Calimalae, II. 4. " Pacta et conventiones que *mercatores*

In England it is probable that the local courts took a more liberal view of informal contracts than did the king's justices. "In London a man shall have a writ of covenant without a deed for covenant broken[1]."

The record of the Fair court of St Ives for 1291 presents several cases of disputed contracts in which the parties differed as to the terms of the contract, but in no case is there any reference to a written agreement. The fair courts may indeed have insisted on formalities of some kind or other, but it would seem that written agreements in such matters as partnership or brokerage were not essential. It is quite clear that in the 14th century the validity of nuda pacta in commercial transactions was recognised in Italy by mercantile usage, and it seems probable that in commercial and local courts they were recognised in England.

In Italy it was not as a rule necessary for merchants to state in written contracts the cause of the obligation. The consuls of the Merchant Gild, declare the statutes of Piacenza for the year 1323, are bound and ought to give and render justice (rationem) to any person on any document made or written by the hand of a merchant that shall say: "ego talis debeo tibi tantam pecuniam sicut facerent

Kallismale fecerint inter se unus alteri seu que aliquis mercator fecerit cum tentoribus vel remendatoribus vel *aliis personis* que huic arti non tenerentur *faciemus inviolabiter observari* excepto de ludo taxillorum."

[1] Pollock, *Contracts*, 141, and Pollock and Maitland, II. 222 and note 2.

et redderent de instrumento publici notarii[1]." These
statutes do not stand alone, and several Italian laws
expressly declare that contracts are to be enforced
though the cause is not stated in the written agreement[2]. The statutes refer as a rule to debts "ex
causa negotiationis," but as they expressly state the
contract is to be enforced, even if no cause of debt is
stated, it was inevitable that in practice a "causa"
was not necessary. The merchants wished for perfect freedom of contract. A vast number of medieval
bonds are extant which contain a simple acknowledgement of the debt, without cause assigned[3]. It
is perhaps impossible to say that in early medieval
times all the trading countries of Western Europe
had gone as far as the great commercial cities of

[1] Stat. Merc. of Placentia 1323, rubric 10.

[2] Capitula de mercatoribus fugitivis of Milan, 1347. "*Etiam si
causa debiti non sit apposita in illa* scriptura, vel alio modo appareat
debitor seu constet de debito, termino solvendi debitum elapso,
teneatur et debeat solvere creditori. Et hoc statutum locum
habeat in contractibus praeteritis, praesentibus et futuris."

Stat. Merc. of Bergamo 1457. St. di San Marino, II. 10.
"Scripturae privatae contra scribentem habeantur in omnia pro
publico instrumento, etiamsi nulla fuerit expressa causa obliga-
tionis."

St. Merc. Brescia, 1429, c. 107. "Quilibet debitor ex causis
mercantiarum factarum alicui mercatori seu personis, dummodo
constet de debito per cartam...seu scripturam manu debitoris...
etiamsi causa debiti non sit apposita in illa scriptura...debeat
solvere..."

Cf. Goldschmidt, 306, note 36. Lattes, 297, note 9. Pertile,
VI. i. 420, note 64.

[2] Des Marez, *Lettres de Foire*, Documents passim, 13th century. *Monumenta Historiae Patriae*, vol. of Cartae, 12th century
passim. Kurze, *Hanseakten aus England*, Documents, 12 (1288),
45 (1311).

Italy in refusing to recognise the necessity of stating
the cause of contracts, but for later times the opinion
of Lord Mansfield, that the purely English doctrine
of "consideration" did not apply to commercial
contracts, is interesting. "A nudum pactum does
not exist in the usage and law of merchants. I take
it that the ancient notion about the want of consideration was for the sake of evidence only—in
commercial cases among merchants the want of
consideration is not an objection."

Though acknowledgements of debts in medieval
times were often short, containing little besides the
amount, the names of creditor and debtor, and the
date and place of payment, the written contract for
commercial transactions had by the 13th century
reached on the continent a high stage of development[1]. "Willingly in order to praise the past has the
remark been made," writes M. Blancard in the
introduction to his edition of a series of more than
one thousand 13th century commercial documents of
Marseilles, "that for our forefathers to establish an
obligation the spoken word sufficed. If they wished
to strengthen the obligation, it was, it has been said,
not by a written act but by shaking hands. This assertion cannot apply to the 13th century as the long list
of documents which I have edited or analysed proves.
Every obligation, even though commercial, was not
then based on the spoken word alone, nor on shaking
hands, nor even on the kiss of peace when it was in
vogue; it was contracted in writing, and not simply
and briefly because that would not have presented

1 Goldschmidt, 151, 152, note 31.

sufficient guarantees, but with a luxury of formulas without connection, or at least out of all proportion with the object of the contract." Though both Church and mercantile usage laid stress upon the binding force of a verbal promise, for the sake of evidence and to prevent misunderstandings contracts were no doubt generally committed to writing. Perhaps the most striking feature in the medieval bonds and contracts is the abundance of clauses safeguarding the interests of the creditor. As a general rule they were in Southern Europe drawn up by public notaries or professional scribes who by the 13th century had become exceedingly numerous and influential. Genoa alone had in the middle of the 13th century 200, Pisa at its close nearly 300, Milan in the following century well over 500, notaries. A single Marseilles notary seems to have drawn up in a single year (1245) more than a thousand commercial documents and on one occasion nearly 60 on a single day[1]. Under the influence of the notaries a uniform legal phraseology—stylus mercatorum—was introduced into the commercial documents of Southern Europe, and this uniformity of language did much to fix and generalise mercantile customs. In many parts of Europe contracts were interpreted by the rules of Roman law, but the universally adopted forms of notarial contracts evaded many of the rules of the law which were not strict enough to satisfy the requirements of the medieval merchant. Almost invariably the debtor

[1] Goldschmidt, 151—2, note 31. Blancard, *Documents Inedits de Marseilles*, Introduction, p. 48.

renounced all the advantages that Roman law conferred upon him: "exceptio non numeratae pecuniae,
exceptio rei venditae non traditae, exceptio doli,
condictio," privileges of women and many others.
Thus in Ypres fair bond (A.D. 1281) the Count of
Flanders in the acknowledgement of a debt to merchants of Sienna renounces "in his omnibus et
singulis supradictis—privilegio fori et crucis, exceptioni doli, condictioni indebiti et sine causa vel
ex injusta causa, convencioni judicum,—omnique
alii juris auxilio canonici et civilis, cunctisque aliis
exceptionibus, constitutionibus, dilationibus, defen-
sionibus, et cujuscunque alterius juris auxiliis":
and in another, two Ypres merchants renounce in
favour of their debtor Bertram de Fort, citizen of
Rochelle, "a tous privileges de Sainte Englise et de‧
croise prise et a prendre et a tous plais de cristiente
et de loi mondaine et a toutes les coses qui dendroit
ce paiement leur poroient eidier et valoir, et le devant
dit Bertram le Fort greveir ou nuire[1]." In the
Marseilles contracts the renunciations are most
numerous and detailed. To England "the Lombard
merchants have brought with them precedents for
bonds, lengthy, precise and stringent forms which
they compel their English debtors to execute[2]." In
England however the continental system of public
notaries never gained a firm footing. The system
had great advantages; the notary[3] was a public

---

[1] Des Marez, *Lettres de Foire à Ypres*, Documents 84 and 46,
cf. Nos. 23, 34, 74, 93, 127, 140, 149, 157.

[2] Pollock and Maitland, I. 219.

[3] Pertile VI. part i. p. 416, note 40, and p. 295. Bresslau, *Urkundenlehre*, traces the institution from late Roman Empire, ch. 8.

official, originally appointed only by Pope or Emperor; when princes, bishops and cities were granted or had usurped the right of appointment, the notary still retained his rank of a public officer. Documents drawn up by a public notary were regarded by the law as authentic[1].

Other means however were available for securing the recognition of contracts and bonds by the public authorities. The "fair bond" seems to have been extremely common in North-Western Europe, and over 7000 of these bonds dating from 1249–1291 have been discovered at Ypres alone. It is probable that until 1275 or thereabouts the Ypres bonds were not drawn up by official scribes, but from 1283 onwards the bonds are the handiwork of a small body of clerks who must have been the clerks of the town. But both before and after this change the bonds were as a rule authentic documents because they were almost invariably drawn up in the presence of the town echevins. The number of the magistrates present varied; it was generally two but occasionally five or six. The fair bond then became a kind of public document. "A proof of the obligation became superfluous; the recognition of the debt before the magistrates gave it full and entire credence,

[1] Bresslau, *Urkundenlehre*, 493: "das Ende der Entwickelung ist, dass die von einem öffentlichen Notar ausgefertigte formell echte Urkunde ein Instrumentum publicum, dass heisst, ein mit publica fides ausgestattetes Aktenstuck wird, das die in ihm aus amtlicher Wahrnehmung bezeugten Thatsachen *unbedingt beweist*."

Pertile, vi. i. p. 417—18 and notes 48—51. Stat. Antiq. Romae, iii. 112, "Nulla persona audeat opponere aliquam exceptionem contra instrumentum scriptum manu notarii Romani."

and no proof could prevail against it[1]." At the great fairs of Champagne the same expedient was adopted and the bonds were passed before the guards of the fair, who impressed them with the fair seal. Originally it was not necessary for fair debts to be so authenticated. The customs of the fair at first allowed anyone to bind himself "en la foire soulz le scel et sans le scel de la foire," and debts contracted during the fair could be proved by witness. "Item au prouver sa debte, faudra instrument scelle du scel desdites foires ou enregistre où registre d'icelles, ou deulx tesmoings qui temoigneront par une voye ou par gaige de bataille[2]." But a desire to avoid frauds, and to increase the revenues of the fairs, led to a change in the law and customs of the Champagne fairs. All bonds for debts contracted during the fairs were to be authenticated by the fair seal. The ordinance of 1349 was most precise and established that "toutes les lecttres touchant le faict et action des foires qui ne seront scellee du scel desdites foires, exceptez les memoriaux et actes des parties tant seulement, soit de nul effect, ny a icelles lettres aucune foi soit adjoustee." Once sealed the bond was valid and could only be repudiated by proving that the fair seal had been forged. "Scel authentique fait foi par la coutume." But for the bonds of the Champagne fairs the seal not only served as a proof of the authenticity of the docu-

---

[1] Des Marez, *op. cit.*, p. 40 and 17 and 13.

[2] The quotations from " Les coustumes, stille et usaige" of the Champagne Fairs are taken from Huvelin, *Droit des Marchés*, 474—8.

ments, it also gave them executive force throughout the French kingdom. Nor was this all. The international importance of the Champagne fairs gave to their bonds a special value, and at Piacenza statutes of 1336 declare that "litterae nundinarum Campanie et Brie" should have the evidential value and the same executive force as public documents[1]. In England the legislation of Edward I. provided a ready and efficient method of authenticating the debts of merchants and securing their payment. Though the two statutes of 1283 and 1285 were not confined to merchants or to debts arising out of mercantile transactions, the preamble to both statutes shows that they were enacted in the interests of the merchant classes ; and in 1311 upon complaint that the statutes, though favourable to the great merchants, were found to press hard upon the people, the regulations of the statutes were limited to contracts between merchants[2]. The two acts are of great importance in the history of the Law Merchant in England. Though enacted in Parliament and intended before their modification in 1311 to apply to debts of every kind throughout the realm, they yet mark a development in the law that was observed in the special commercial courts and enforced in the case of commercial debt. The use of English statute law, and the frequent employment that has been made of the statutes and customs of individual cities as evidence for the rules of Law Merchant which has

[1] Huvelin, p. 480.

[2] Kurze, *Hanseakten aus England* (Hansische Geschichtsquellen, Band vi.), Introduction, pp. 28, 29.

been declared to be distinct from the common law, may perhaps require explanation.

The Law Merchant was no doubt a special body of law. It was the law observed by merchants, to a large extent created by them, and distinct in England from the common law of the land and from the usages and customs of individual cities. Of this there can be no doubt and it is recognised in the most unmistakable terms by the Statute of the Staple of Edward III.'s reign which ordains (cap. 8) "that all merchants coming to the Staple, their servants and their meiny in the Staple shall be ruled by the law merchant in all things touching the Staple and not by the common law of the land, nor by the usage of boroughs, cities and other towns." But though the Law Merchant was thus a separate system of law, distinct from the common law, distinct from individual town customs, it was by means of the central authority that the law was sometimes altered or authoritatively declared; and while it cannot be asserted that a commercial usage of any individual town, however great or however important that town might be, formed a rule of the Law Merchant, the usages of the great commercial cities tended to conform to the general usage of merchants throughout Europe. The Law Merchant of medieval times was the system of rules actually enforced in the commercial courts and actually observed by merchants in their dealings with one another, just as Modern International Law is the system of rules actually observed by modern States in the relations of State to State. The treaties, the legislation, and the actions of individual States do not necessarily conform to the generally recognised rules of International Law, but they may be and are used as evidence to establish what those rules really are. In the same way the Statute Law of medieval states, the ordinances of medieval kings, and the usages of medieval law, need not conform, in any particular case, to the commercial regulations generally enforced among medieval merchants, but they may be used to establish the general usages of merchants in commercial cases. Both International Law and the Law Merchant are from their very nature vague and uncertain. In modern times great nations have held views diametrically opposed upon the rules of International Law in not unimportant matters. In medieval times the merchants were not rarely at a loss when called upon to declare the law, and occasionally craved time for consideration. For the rules of International Law and of the Law Merchant depend mainly upon the general practice; and if with numberless treatises on International Law the international rule even in modern times can often only be regarded as a moot question, there can be no wonder if the medieval merchant was at times uncertain as to the rule of the Law Merchant. To a modern enquirer the task of determining what is a general principle of the Law Merchant and what is merely a local or national usage is far more difficult than it was to the medieval merchant in a medieval court. The attempt however has to be made, and everything that throws light upon the commercial customs and usages of the time has to be taken into consideration. The commercial statutes of any individual country or city are not the Law Merchant, but that law at times found expression in those statutes. The usages of any particular town never conformed entirely to the usages generally observed in every country; but collectively the customs of the great commercial cities of Europe form valuable material from which may be deduced by careful comparison what were probably the general usages. Moreover while the Law Merchant was in its broadest sense the body of commercial rules observed throughout Western Christendom, it must be remembered that each country developed to a certain extent upon its own lines. There is a sense in which an "English Law Merchant" may be said to have existed. The Law Merchant as observed in England was always slowly changing; often that change was due to the influence of changes that had taken place in the commercial usages of other countries and was effected by decisions in the special commercial courts in fairs or staple town or seaport where foreign merchants abounded and had a right to express their views of the law, forming half of or all the "mercati" of the court when a foreigner is a party, or the case is between foreigners: sometimes on the other hand the change was effected by royal authority, and it was by royal authority that the English system of recognition and enforcement of debt was brought into closer harmony with the usages and laws that already prevailed on the continent. "Bonds of record," a speedy process of execution, and the liability of the debtor's property

8—2

both real and personal, were recognised maxims in the continental countries of Western Europe, and these were the maxims enforced by Edward's legislation of 1283 and 1285. "Forasmuch," declares the statute of Acton Burnell of the year 1283, "Merchants which heretofore have lent their goods to divers persons be greatly impoverished because there is no speedy Law provided for them to have recovery of their debts at the day of payment assigned, and by reason hereof many merchants have withdrawn to come into this realm with their merchandises, to the damage as well of the merchants as of the whole realm, the king by himself and by his council hath ordained and established, That the Merchant which will be sure of his debt shall cause his debtor to come before the Mayor of London, or of York, or Bristol, or before the Mayor and a clerk which the king shall appoint for the same, for to knowledge the debt and the day of payment, and the recognisance shall be entered into a roll with the hand of the said clerk, which shall be known. Moreover the said clerk shall make with his own hand a Bill Obligatory whereunto the seal of the debtor shall be put with the king's seal, that shall be provided for the same purpose, the which seal shall remain in the keeping of the Mayor and clerk aforesaid. And if the debtor doth not pay at the day to him limited, the creditor may come before the said Mayor and clerk with his Bill Obligatory, and if it be found by the roll and by the bill that the debt was knowledged and that the day of payment is expired, the Mayor shall incontinent cause the moveables of the debtor to be sold, as far as the debt doth amount by the praising of honest men, as Chattels and Burgages devisable until the whole sum of the debt, and the money without delay shall be paid to the creditor. And if the Mayor can find no buyer, he shall cause the moveables to be delivered to the creditor at a reasonable price, as much as doth amount to the sum of the debt in allowance of his debt. And the king's seal shall be put unto the sale and deliverance of the Burgages devisable for a perpetual witness. And if the debtor have no moveables within the jurisdiction of the Mayor whereupon the debt may be levied, but have some otherwhere within the realm, then shall the Mayor send the recognisance made before him and the clerk aforesaid unto the chancellor under the king's seal. And the chancellor shall direct a writ unto the sheriff in whose bailiwick the moveables of the debtor be, and the sheriff shall cause him to agree with his creditor in such form as the Mayor should have done in case the moveables of the debtor had been within his power. And let them that praise the moveable goods to be delivered unto the creditor take good heed that they do set a reasonable price upon them; for if they do set an overhigh price for favour born to the debtor and to the damage of the creditor, then shall the thing so praised be delivered unto themselves at such price as they have limited, and they shall forthwith be answerable unto the creditor for his debt. And if the debtor have no moveables whereupon his debt may be levied, then shall his body be taken where it may be found and kept in prison until he have made agreement, or his friends for him." Two years later the regulations of the law of 1283 were reenacted and in addition the immoveable property of the debtor was made liable. "And within a quarter of a year after that he is taken," ordains the statute of 1285, "his chattels and lands shall be delivered to him so that by his own he may levy and pay his debt. And it shall be lawful unto him during the same quarter to sell his lands and tenements for the discharge of his debts, and his sale shall be good and effectual. And if he do not agree within the quarter, next after the quarter expired, all the lands and goods of the debtor shall be delivered unto the merchant by a reasonable extent to hold them until such time as the debt is levied....And the merchant shall have such seisin in the lands and tenements delivered unto him or his assignee that he may maintain a writ of Novel Disseisin if he is put out....And if in case the sheriff return that the debtor cannot be found or that he is clerk, the merchant shall have writs to all the sheriffs where he shall have land....And a seal shall be provided that shall serve for fairs and the same shall be sent unto every fair." Similarly the Ordinance of the Staple (1353) gave power to the Mayor of the staple "to take recognisances of debts which a man will make him," "to the intent that contracts made within the same staple shall be the better holden and the payments readily made[1]." The procedure was however made somewhat more severe; execution

---

[1] Keble, cap. 9.

was to proceed "in manner as it is contained in the
Statute Merchant" (1285), but the debtor was to
"have no advantage of the quarter of a year which
is contained in the said Statute Merchant."

Originally immoveables had not in Germanic law
been liable for debt. This principle of Germanic law
was already losing ground in the times of the
Carlovingians[1], and in Italy[2], France and Germany[3]
the lands of a debtor were by the 13th century liable
as a general rule for the debts of their owner, though
in many cases they could only be seized after the

[1] Brunner, *Deutsche Rechtsgeschichte*, II. 459, 460; in note 20
(p. 460) Brunner refers to a charter cited in note 41 on p. 74 as
the plainest evidence "dass die Entstehung der Immobiliarexe-
cution in der Konfiskation friedlosen Gutes ihren rechtgeschicht-
lichen Ausgangspunkt hatte."

Cf. Pertile, VI. ii. p. 330.

[2] v. Pertile, VI. ii. 331. On p. 338 and 339, notes 55 and 56,
Pertile quotes *inter alia* the following: Const. leg. Pisanae Civitatis (A.D. 1231). "Data la sentenza, si apud reum, vel alium
pro eo, res ipsa mobilis vel immobilis invenitur, per consulem
justitie victori, et in ipsius potestatem statim tribuatur."

Stat. of Vercelli, A.D. 1241. "Si quis ad postulationem
creditoris consignaverit bona sua et de rebus mobilibus non
consignavit tantum unde possit satisfieri creditoribus, tunc de
rebus immobilibus...satisfaciat creditoribus ejus...."

[3] Stadtrecht Münster-Bielefeld (circa 1221), cap. 44. Keutgen,
Urkunden, p. 153. "Si quis obtinuerit sentenciis, quod debet
ostendere res de quibus debitor suus ei possit solvere, non licet ei
ostendere super vestes suas et sue uxoris et ejus suppelectilem,
si habet wicbelethe (*i.e.* lands held by burgage tenure) vel alias
res."

In Hamburg the landed property of citizens was by Stadtrecht
of 1262 (c. 22) made liable for debt. See *Das Handlungsbuch*,
'Vickos von Geldersen,' edited by Norrnheim, Introduction,
p. xxx.

Schroeder, *Rechtsgeschichte*, p. 767.

moveables had been taken and found insufficient. The process of change was slow and during the period of transformation the usage varied in different parts of the same kingdom. In several provinces, writes Viollet in his History of French Law, "in the 12th and sometimes even in the 13th century the movable property of the debtor alone was liable for his obligations." In Belgium[1] "immoveables were often pledged as a security in commercial transactions." The whole tendency of mercantile usage was to secure the creditor in every way possible. This tendency is not only seen in the introduction of a prompt process of execution and the liability of landed property for the payment of debt: it also appears in the solidarity stipulated in mercantile contracts for sureties and in cases where there were several principal debtors. Among the thousands of fair bonds discovered at Ypres there are but few in which debtors are bound only for their own part, and when this is the case the responsibility of each debtor is defined most scrupulously. As a general rule where there is more than one debtor in these bonds[2] the debtors bind themselves "chascun por le tout," and when there were several sureties in the same way each was surety for the whole debt[3].

---

[1] Des Marez, *La Lettre de Foire*, pp. 40—52. Des Marez, *La Propriété Foncière dans les Villes du Moyen Age*, pp. 252, 253.

[2] Des Marez, *La Lettre de Foire*, pp. 40—42 and documents, nos. 9, 10, 11, 13, 17, 23, 40, 43, 46, 64, 74, 82, 94, 118, 121, 131, 153, 154.

[3] Des Marez, nos. 8, 18, 43, 44 B, 53, 55, 61, 64, 70, 83, 88, 89, 92, 94, 99, 105, 109, 118, 120, 139.

There is the same solidarity[1] of creditor in the commercial documents of Italy, of Marseilles and numerous
other towns, and the formularies in the " summa artis
notariae" of Rolandinus, a work which exercised a vast
influence upon the form of legal documents throughout the Middle Ages, contains the customary formula,
" unusquisque ipsorum principaliter et in solidum sine
aliqua exceptione juris." But mercantile practice
went further than this in the early Middle Ages. A
merchant was held responsible in other cities and in
other lands for the debts of his fellow townsman.
The usage however ran counter to the real interests
of the trading classes, and a series of laws, ordinances,
royal charters, and treaties gradually abolished this
burdensome custom. Early in his reign Edward I.
declared that the rule should not apply to English
merchants in English cities and fairs, and the
Ordinance of the Staple issued in the middle of the
reign of Edward III. extended the privilege, though
with a saving clause that may have robbed it of
much of its value, to foreign merchants. The 17th
chapter of this ordinance declares " that no merchant
stranger be impeached for another's trespass or for
another's debt whereof he is not debtor, pledge nor
mainpernour, provided always that if our liege people,
merchants or other, be indamaged by any lords of
strange lands or their subjects, and the said lords
duly required fail of right to our said subjects, we
shall have the law of Marque and the taking of them

[1] See references in Goldschmidt, p. 309, note 41, and p. 284
and notes. Among these are the English bonds published by
Bond in *Archaeologia*, vol. xxviii. (London, 1840).

again, as hath been used in times passed without fraud or deceit." The same tendency was evident in other countries. " In 1193 Philip Augustus takes under his protection the merchants of Ypres and their merchandise throughout the extent of his realm. In future they cannot be arrested either for the debts of their fellow citizens or for those of the Court of Flanders, unless they had become sureties[1]." Queen Elizabeth of Hungary[2], in consequence of the complaints of the merchants of Vienna and Austria, promised in a royal charter of the year 1381 that when Austrian merchants came into Hungary for purposes. of trade they should not be arrested and condemned for the debts and misdeeds of others. In Italy a long series of treaties between the great commercial cities attempted during the 13th century to limit this right of reprisal, and of this policy Florence made itself the leader during the 14th century[3]. The statutes of the important Calimala gild (1301) instructed the consuls to call as quickly as they could a special council, or if they preferred, a general council, " and to take counsel with them as to what was to be done with the cases of reprisals in divers lands in which our merchants

---

[1] Des Marez, *La Lettre de Foire*, p. 43.

[2] *Quellen zur Geschichte der Stadt Wien*, II. i. number 1002.

[3] See Bonolis, *La Giurisdizione della Mercanzia in Firenze nel secolo xiv.*, especially pp. 96 and 97.

Del Vecchio, *Le Rappresaglie nei Comuni Medievali specialmente in Firenze*, especially pp. 230—252 and the documents in appendices.

Arias, *I Trattati Commerciali della Repubblica Fiorentina*, pp. 156—229, and documents in Appendix.

often suffer loss." "They shall take good heed," the statute continues, "that the reprisals are settled, and that all the citizens of Florence by reason of whom reprisals have been granted against other citizens shall effectually be compelled to give satisfaction so that the men of Florence do not suffer further loss." "The consuls moreover are in duty bound to assemble and meet with the captains of the seven greater gilds and petition...that it may be established by the council of the commune of Florence that no reprisal be granted or conceded to any person on behalf of the commune of Florence save in the presence of the seven captains[1]." A few years later the councillors of the Mercanzia were ordered to arrange with the authorities of the city that "treaties be made with any land and community of Tuscany or elsewhere as might seem good to the five councillors that as between the commune of Florence and the said communes reprisals cannot and shall not be granted or conceded for any cause save in case of robbery only[2]." During the course of the 15th century reprisals against merchants were rapidly growing rarer, and in 1474 the Emperor ordered the restoration of goods taken by way of reprisal from a Jew, while Henry V. of England declared any unjust aggression against foreigners high treason[3]. The system of reprisals forms part both of the Law Merchant and of "Private International Law." It forms

---

[1] St. Calimalae (1301), Lb. iv. c. 30.

[2] Statuto della Mercanzia del 1312. Rubrics 6, 14, 23 printed in Del Vecchio.

[3] Pertile, I. p. 265, note 67, and Del Vecchio, pp. 87, 88.

part of the Law Merchant in that the system was recognised and enforced in the special commercial courts of the Middle Ages, and because it corresponded to the peculiar character of commercial enterprise during early medieval times when towns and their gilds formed close economic units, united for purposes of trade, supporting their members against other cities in their just demands and consequently held liable, and at first justly held liable, for the misdeeds and debts of their own citizens and members. The communal spirit which was so strong was evident in other ways, and townsman or gildsman had a right to a share in any bargain made in his presence[1]. This spirit was however growing antiquated, and the growth of the principle that the merchant was not liable for the debts of his fellow citizens but only for those for which he had become surety, marks a distinct advance alike in the Law Merchant and in International Law.

During the Middle Ages contracts of partnership were common, and at their close companies with freely alienable shares had come into existence. In the early centuries the most common form of partnership was the "commenda." This was a partnership in which one of the parties supplied the capital either in the shape of money or goods, without personally taking an active part in the operations of the society, while the other party supplied none or only a smaller fraction of the capital and conducted the actual trade

---

[1] Bateson, *Records of Leicester*, p. xxxii. and p. 271.

Faigniez, *Documents relatifs à l'histoire de l'industrie et du commerce en France*, vol. I. No. 210 (Paris), vol. II. No. 71.

of the association. This form of partnership was especially used in maritime trade and was often confined to single ventures. Its popularity was due to the fact that it enabled the capitalist to turn his money to good account without violating the canonical laws against usury, and the small merchant or shipper to secure credit and to transfer the risk of the venture to the capitalist. The nature of the contract will best be shown by quoting one or two examples of the vast number of these contracts that have been preserved.

The following is a Marseilles contract of the year 1210 :

"Notum sit cunctis quod ego Bonetus Pellicerius confiteor et recognosco me habuisse et recepisse in comanda, a te Stephano de Mandoil et a te Bernardo Baldo, xxv l. regalium coronatorum...quas ego portabo ad laborandum in hoc itinere Bogie, in nave de Estella, vel ubicumque navis ierit causa negotiandi, ad vestrum proficuum et meum, ad fortunam dei et ad usum maris, et totum lucrum et capitale convenio et promitto reducere in potestatem vestri et vestrorum fideliter, et veritatem inde vobis dicam, et ita hoc me observaturum in mea bona fide per stipulationem promitto, et in omni lucro quod Deus ibi dederit, debeo habere et accipere quartum denarium[1]."

Such contracts were not rare in Italy in the 12th

[1] *Documents Inédits sur le Commerce de Marseilles au Moyen Age*, by Blancard, Document 4, vol. i. p. 7. There are scores of similar contracts of Commenda in these two volumes, and there are numerous 12th century examples in the volume of Chartae in the *Monumenta Historiae Patriae*.

century and the contracts are to the same intent as those of Marseilles in the 13th century. " March 1155. Ego Petrus de Tolosi profiteor me accepisse a te Ottone Bono libras centum viginti septem quas debeo portare laboratum Salernum vel ex hinc apud Siceliam, et de proficuo quod ibi deus dederit debeo habere quartam et reditum debeo mittere in tua potestate[1]."

Often when both parties to the contract contributed to the capital of the association the partnership was termed "collegantia," or "societas" to distinguish it from the more common form of commenda in which the commendator alone supplied the funds.

"Bonus Johannes Malfuastus et Bonus Senior Rubeus contraxerunt societatem, in quam Bonus Johannes libras 34 et Bonus Senior libras 16 contulit. Hanc societatem portare debet Alexandriam laboratum nominatus Bonus Senior et inde Januam venire debet. Capitali extracto proficuum et persone (?) per medium. Ultra confessus est nominatus Bonus Senior quod portat de rebus nominati Boni Johannis libr. 20 sol. 13 de quibus debet habere quartam proficui—. Juravit insuper ipse Bonus Senior quod supradictam societatem et commendacionem diligenter salvabit et promovebit societatem ad proficuum sui et Boni johannis et commendacionem ad proficuum ipsius Boni johannis et quod societatem omnem et ipsam commendacionem et proficuum in potestatem reducet ipsius Boni Johannis[2]."

---

[1] *Monumenta Historiae Patriae*, Chartae, column 287.

[2] Goldschmidt, p. 260 and note 88 b.

But whether the commendator alone or both parties contributed to the capital, the association remained essentially of the same character. The commendator in both cases was a kind of sleeping partner, and it was left to the "tractator" to carry out all the necessary operations. Though the partnership was generally formed for the purpose of a definite speculation, it was also formed for an indefinite series of commercial transactions, or for an indefinite or sometimes a definite time, which was occasionally as long as 10 years[1].

As a rule the commendator who supplied the capital took the risk of the transaction; if the goods were lost he could not recover the amount he had advanced, provided that the contract contained the usual clause "ad risicum et fortunam Dei, maris et gentium," or its equivalent. The usual share in the profits of a tractator who brought no capital into the partnership was a quarter, while in the case where he contributed to the general fund, his share of the profits amounted to a half. It is hard to tell whether the "tractator" in early times always traded in his own name, though there is no doubt that in later times he did[2]. Pertile holds the view that originally the tractator was regarded as a mere factor of the commendator who was responsible for the acts of the tractator, but that gradually in the course of time the principle was established that he was only responsible to the amount of the capital

[1] Goldschmidt, p. 264.
[2] Goldschmidt, p. 265 and note 104. Lattes, p. 157.

which he had advanced[1]. In Florence this principle
was definitely established by statute in 1408. In
the medieval commenda was represented both the
dormant partner and the principle of limited
liability of modern times. The commenda was not
confined to England: it existed during the Middle
Ages in Germany and Scandinavia[2]. In cases where
there were several commendators who entrusted
their capital to one or more tractators, the latter
began to assume a more independent position towards
commendators. Contracting in their own name the
managers were responsible for the debts of the
association, while the commendators were freed, in
Florence as early as 1408, from all liability beyond
the amount of their quota. This type of commenda
was a natural development of the simple original
type in which there were but two persons involved,
—a single commendator who advanced the capital to a
single tractator; but it was an important development,
and in the 16th century it was regulated in Italy by
several city statutes and in the following century in
France by regulation[3]. Thus regulated the society
contained both members with limited liability and
members with unlimited liability, and it was the
latter that controlled the administration of the
society. The older and simpler form of commenda,

[1] Pertile, IV. 685, 686, note 24. Cf. Viollet, *Histoire du droit
civil français*, p. 762. "Dans la société le bailleur de fonds ou
commendataire n'est passible des pertes que jusqu'à concurrence
des fonds qu'il a mis ou dû mettre dans la société."

[2] Norrnheim, *Geldersen's Handlungsbuch*, Introduction, 43—5.
Amira, *Nordgermanisches Obligationesrecht*, vol. II.

[3] Goldschmidt, 269. Lattes, p. 162 and notes.

however, existed side by side with the newer and
more complex type. Of the newer type the modern
"Société en commandite" is the historical descendant
and it is characterised by the same essential features,
the existence of two classes of members, the one with
a responsibility limited to the amount of the capital
they have contributed, and the other with an
unlimited liability for the debts of the society, the
administration of which lies solely in their hands[1].
On the other hand the commendator of the older
and simple type of commenda has his counterpart in
the dormant partner of modern commercial law.

But side by side with the commenda there
existed throughout the Middle Ages a closer kind
of partnership in which the partners were normally
coordinate members of the association with the same
privileges and responsibilities. The usual expression
for this type of society was "compagnia" or "societas,"
and the firm was generally designated by the name
of one of its members with the addition of the phrase
"et socii," or the like. It became an essential feature
of this form of partnership that the partners were all
of them responsible individually for the debts of the
firm[2]. At no time in Italy was the power of partners
to bind by contract their fellow partners in practice
denied[3]. The principle of direct representation was
thus admitted, and Baldo writing in the 14th century
declared "ex consuetudine mercatorum unus socius
scribit nomen alterius[4]." Baldo however adds that

[1] V. Thaller, *Traité Élémentaire de Droit Commercial*, §§ 258—
262, pp. 160—162.
[2] Lattes, p. 161 and notes. [3] Cf. however pp. 132—135 below.
[4] Goldschmidt, p. 276, note 139.

M. 9

this was "abusio." This was an important advance
upon the principles of both Roman and old Germanic
law, neither of which recognised sufficiently the
principle of direct representation. "All this view
of the law," says Kohler writing of the principle
of representation, "appears altogether artificial and
cannot well appeal to primitive man: he cannot
understand a transaction (based) upon the will of
another; even a developed law like Roman law has
only developed 'representation' very imperfectly and
German law long resisted it[1]." Medieval merchants
and mercantile usage recognised the principle of
representation; they recognised it not only in the
right of one partner to make contracts binding upon
the other partners of a firm, they also recognised it
in the medieval bills of exchange with their clauses
to order or bearer.

As the names of all the partners did not appear[2]
in the name of the firm, but were simply referred
to generally in the phrase "et socii" or some equivalent expression, it became important to determine

[1] Kohler, 'Zivilrecht' in *Holtzendorff's Encyklopädie der Rechtswissenschaft*, vol. I. p. 598. Kohler quotes from and refers to
many Italian authorities of 12—14th century on representation.
Among them St. Como (A.D. 1232). "Tantum valeat et prosit illi,
ad cujus partem vel cujus nomine facta est vel recepta, ac si illam
cartam vel contractum vel obligationem recepisset."

St. of Brescia, regulation of A.D. 1252 in St. of 1313. "Quod ex
omni contractu inito et facto nomine alterius, tam de mercato quam
de aliis rebus, acquiratur actio et acquisita sit illi vel illis, quorum
vel cujus nomine contractus sive promissio factus est vel facta."

[2] Bartolus. "Secundum consuetudinem et fere totius Italiae—
litteris mercatorum unus nominatur nomine proprio et omnes alii
nomine appellativo, hoc modo: Titius et socius talis societatis,"
quoted by Goldschmidt, p. 276, note 137.

who were to be legally regarded as members of the firm. In early Italian statutes actual common trading of the persons concerned, or general notoriety, sufficed to prove the partnership: "et intellegantur socii qui in eadem statione vel negotiatione morantur vel mercantur ad invicem[1]." In doubtful cases the books of the firm were consulted[2]. But general notoriety and the books of the firm were not found sufficient either to protect the general public against partners who denied the partnership altogether or who asserted that the partnership had been dissolved, or to protect merchants from a general liability for all the debts of a trader with whom they occasionally combined for the purpose of a common speculation. Dissolution of partnerships was to be valid only if effected "per instrumentum publicum." If any one practising in the Calimala craft," says a Florentine gild statute of 1301, "or having a share in any 'societas' of that craft has renounced or shall renounce it in the future, such renunciation shall not be valid nor be admitted by the consuls, unless he shall show that he withdrew from that firm by means of a public document, and the consuls shall have that document published throughout the whole craft." Registration of partners became usual; from the 14th century onwards such registers were kept not merely by the gilds but by the city authorities;

[1] St. Mutinae, 1327, quoted among others by Goldschmidt, 276, notes 140 and 141.

[2] St. of Calimala of Florence, Lb. ii. rubric 43. "*Si quis... librum corporis sue societatis celavit vel celaverit ita quod haberi et videri non possit quod sit sotii* (sic) *dicte societatis.*" Cf. Lattes, p. 174, note 59 and p. 283.

and the registration required, as a rule, "the direct intervention either personally or by special procuration of all the members of the firm[1]."

It has been stated that one partner could represent the rest and make contracts binding upon the whole firm, and that this was an advance upon the principles of Roman and Germanic law, which only recognised representation to a limited degree. But though a single partner could thus represent the firm, originally it was as a rule only in virtue of special procuration that he was privileged so to do. In the medieval contracts of partnership the partners often gave one another by procuration the right to represent and bind the firm. In the absence of such clauses in the contract creditors of the firm for a debt contracted by an individual partner could in some places only make good their claim against the firm as a whole, if the debt had been recognised as a debt of the firm, as by entry in the firm's book, or employment of the money or goods for the common purposes of the firm. Simply in his capacity as partner a merchant had not everywhere in the early centuries of the Middle Ages a right to bind his copartners. "Whoever in the city or district of Florence," declares a Florence gild regulation of the year 1236, " has sold cloth or other things pertaining to trade to any one of this gild cannot seek nor sue for the money or price of the sale from any of the partners of the buyer, or from any one of his firm, unless the money shall be found written in the books of the buyer's firm as payable for the price of that

[1] Lattes, p. 162 and note 68.

sale[1]." Similarly the gild statute of Verona for the
year 1318 required the tacit consent of the other
partners or an express promise on their part to pay
—"nec praejudicet etiam stando in statione et essendo
socius palam; dummodo non esset praesens cum
socio ad accipiendam mercandiam et non promitteret
de solvendo eam."

As late as the 15th century the jurist Alexander
Tartagnus denies the responsibility of the other
partners, unless the contract had been made with
full powers "nomine societatis[2]." Slowly however
the principle gained ground that a partner had as
partner the right to make contracts binding upon
his firm. In all probability this change was due to
the frequency with which the individual partner was
entrusted with this power by special procuration.
Thus in one of the Marseilles documents of the 13th
century which have been already referred to, two
partners concede full powers to the third. "Nos
Dietavivo Alberto et Guidaloto Guidi, Senenses
facimus, constituimus, ordinamus, Bellinchonum
Charrenconi, consocium nostrum, absentem, nostrum
certum et generalem procuratorem in omnibus

---

1 St. of Calimala, 1301, Lb. ii. rubric 19. The date 1236 is
given in the rubric.

2 Goldschmidt, 281, note 154. Goldschmidt gives many
quotations from and references to city and gild statutes, *inter
alia* St. of Calimala Gild (1341). "E niuno mercantante di
questa arte possa obligare in Firenze o nel distretto la sua
compagnia o alcuno compagno della sua compagnia—se non in
debiti o cose che fossono scritte nel libro o libri della sua
compagnia, o se almeno due o più de' compagni non fossono
insieme a tale obligazione fare, o se non avese in ciò speciale
o generale procurazione e mandato da' suoi compagni."

nostris negotiis peragendis,......promittentes nos ratum perpetuo habitaturos quicquid cum eo vel per eum actum fuerit in praemissis, sub obligacione omnium bonorum meorum praesentium et futurorum[1]." Such procurations were exceedingly common[2], and the great Calimala Gild of Florence went so far as to instruct (1301) all its members when they sent any one abroad to transact business to provide them with a special or general procuration. The result was that in actual practice the partner did have power to bind the firm, and that gradually this power was regarded as a matter of course. During the 14th and 15th centuries numerous Italian statutes recognised the responsibility of the other partners for the debts and contracts made by an individual member of the firm. But both the doctrine of the great civil jurists and the decisions of isolated commercial courts were long opposed to this new view of the position of the partner. Thus the decisions of the " Rota of Genoa " only go so far as to say that whatever is written by one of them having the " facultas " of using the name of the firm is said to be written by the firm itself, while another decision declares most plainly that such " facultas " is not to be taken as a matter of course. By the 17th century however the power of an individual partner, though without special procuration, to act in the name of his firm was admitted by the civil jurists[3]. The unlimited

[1] Blancard, *op. cit.*, no. 115.

[2] See numerous quotations and references in Goldschmidt, p. 282, note 155.

[3] De Luca, *De Camb.*, disc. 29, nos. 3, 4, quoted Goldschmidt, p. 283.

liability of the partner for the debts of the firm was, like the right of the partner as partner to represent the firm, of gradual growth, and was not in the early centuries of the Middle Ages universally enforced by the law[1]. In medieval contracts unlimited liability was indeed often stipulated and was in some places a maxim of the law : in the fairs of Champagne, for example, the unlimited responsibility of partners was under certain conditions expressly recognised ; the "usage of the fairs" declared that a partner "oblige tous leurs biens (*i.e.* the partners) pour cause de l'administration qu'il a et qu'il semble avoir, et plus, se aulcun des compaignons se boute en franchise ou destourne ses biens ou les biens de sa compagnye, il est oblige et tout li autre compaignon qui paravant .cette fuite ou tel destournement des biens n'estoient obligez en corps et en biens par la coustume, stille et usaige des foires notoires[2]." It was not however till towards the close of the 16th century that the solidarity of partners was in Italy generally recognised. "Only gradually and without the support of positive law the liability of every partner 'in solidum' came through mercantile usage to be enforced in statutes and judicial decisions. This liability was repeatedly recognised in the decisions of Genoa. Since that time it was never a matter of doubt[3]," and in the 17th century the jurist Ansaldus who, as auditor of the Roman Rota, must have had a

---

[1] Goldschmidt, pp. 284 and 288 and note 159.

[2] Goldschmidt, 285, note 160.

[3] Endemann, *Studien in der romanisch-kanonistischen Wirtschafts- und Rechtslehre*, vol. i. p. 395.

thorough acquaintance with judicial decisions in commercial cases, recognised this unlimited liability and declared that in the first place the creditor had recourse to the capital of the firm, and only in the second place could he avail himself of the unlimited liability of the individual partner[1]. The commenda and the societas had an independent origin and an independent development. Originally the commenda was a purely speculative enterprise, confined mainly at first to maritime trade in which one partner found all or most of the capital and the other traded in his own name. The societas on the other hand had its root in the more permanent association of the family or of persons who had full confidence in each other for the purpose of carrying on, in common, industrial and commercial enterprises in city or town. Both extended the scope of their application, commendas were formed for inland trade and partnerships of the collective type for maritime commerce. Each however developed on its own lines. In the commenda, where from the first the capitalist must have as a rule remained unknown to the merchants who traded with the active partner, the limited liability of the capitalist and the unlimited liability of the active partner were before long firmly established, while in the open " societas " the right of the individual partner to represent and bind the firm on the one hand, and on the other his unlimited liability for its debts, were finally recognised. Both types, modified in points of detail, have passed into modern commercial life. If the commenda has

[1] Endemann, *op. cit.*, pp. 395—6 and 55, 56.

developed into the "Société en commandite," the "societas" has its historical counterpart in the modern "Société en nom collectif" and the Offene Gesellschaft.

A third type of partnership, that of joint-stock companies with the capital in the shape of freely alienable shares, with a liability limited to the amount of capital represented by the share, and with an administrative governing body composed of shareholders in which the majority decided, was in process of formation during the Middle Ages.

To the origin of this type of partnership many causes contributed, but the decisive cause was the growth of colonial enterprises in Italy in the 15th century, and in Holland, France and England in the 16th and 17th centuries. A recent German writer[1] has attributed a great influence upon the birth and development of these companies to a peculiar form of partnership with limited liability that in shipping enterprises was common both in Northern and Southern Europe during the earlier part of the Middle Ages. At Amalfi, for example, in the 11th century the owners, the captain, and even the common sailors all had a share in the profits of the voyage and formed an association whose liability was strictly limited[2]. But it can hardly be said that the adoption of this peculiar form of partnership had a great influence upon the formation of joint-

[1] Lehmann, *Geschichtliche Entwickelung des Aktienrechts* (1895). *Das Recht der Aktienegesellschaften* (1898).

See Thaller, *La Société par Actions dans l'Ancienne France*, pp. 14, 15. Thaller, *Traité Élémentaire de Droit Commercial*, p. 163 note.

[2] Wagner, *Seerecht*, pp. 8, 9. Thaller, *Société par Action*, p. 15.

stock enterprises. No doubt it offered an example of a partnership with limited liability, but so did the far more common commenda; and the essence of a joint-stock company does not consist in the principle of limited responsibility, but rather in the prolongation of the corporate existence and organisation of the company beyond the life of its members and in the free negotiability of the shares.

Of greater influence were the public loans[1] raised by Italian cities during the 13th and following centuries. The loans were divided into shares (luoghi) and the names of the owners were registered in special books. The shares not only passed to the heirs in case of the owner's death, but could be freely bought and sold; and as negotiable shares, even though they cannot in any sense be regarded as shares in a commercial speculation, they showed the keen commercial mind of the Italian an expedient that might be adopted for raising capital for commercial as well as for military purposes. It was in Genoa that the first joint-stock companies arose. To cover the cost of the conquest of Chios and Phocaea (1346) a loan was raised by the Genoan state and as usual was divided into shares of 100 lires, and the shareholders were given the "dominium utile" of the conquered lands. This Colonial company, incorporated with the bank of St George in 1513, continued to exploit the resources of the two islands until their conquest by the Turks in the 16th century. Far more important however was the founding of the great bank of St George in 1407 when the various state

[1] Pertile, II. i. pp. 508—510. Goldschmidt, 292.

loans were consolidated into a single state debt. As security for the interest the city granted important privileges to the holders of the new consolidated stock, which was divided into shares of 100 lires. The stockholders were granted the right (1408) to carry on banking business, and especially after 1453 the administration and exploitation of important Genoan colonies passed into their hands. The creditors of the Genoan state had become the shareholders of a great colonial company which ultimately governed and administered Corsica, Kaffa and the greater part of the foreign dominions of Genoa[1].

Colonial expansion in England, France and Holland led, though much later, to the creation of companies similar to that of Genoa. The Compagnie des Iles d'Amerique, which seems to be the earliest example in France, was created in 1626 and was rapidly followed by others of the same type[2]. The Dutch East India Company (1602) was but little earlier. In England the East India Company[3] received a royal charter in the opening year of the 17th century. At first the company could hardly be considered as a joint-stock company; for in the early years of its history the voyages were separate and not necessarily permanent ventures of the sub-

[1] Pertile, II. i. p. 509.

[2] Viollet, *op. cit.*, p. 767. Thaller, *Société par Actions*, p. 5, says "on ne doit pas remonter plus haut que le règne de Henri IV.": but he gives no example for this earlier date.

[3] Article on East India Company in Palgrave's *Dictionary of Political Economy*.

Levi, *History of British Commerce*, pp. 233, 337 and note.

scribers, who contributed varying amounts to the capital required for the expedition and received a proportionate share of the proceeds when the expedition returned. A shareholder in one of the early expeditions might or might not be a shareholder in the next. In 1613 the first so-called joint-stock was subscribed, but the term is misleading, it was not a subscription of permanent capital. As late as the middle of the 17th century subscribers wished to carry on separate trade in ships of their own, but the company protested and in 1654 a decision of the council of state was given "in favour of joint-stock management and exclusive trading."

It would seem that joint-stock companies took their rise owing to colonial expansion in Italy at the close of the Middle Ages, and had spread to Holland, France and England by the 17th century. The history of the development[1] and of the gradual extension of this form of partnership from projects of colonisation to commercial undertakings of every kind and variety lies outside the scope of this essay. But it is interesting to note that that system of partnership that now controls most of the great commercial and industrial enterprises of modern life, that has popularised and democratised capital and enabled the savings of the people as a whole to be applied to commercial speculations, great and small, of every kind, and that has changed the whole nature of commercial finance, was in its origin the outcome of state necessities and of colonial expansion.

[1] Especially interesting seems the combination of the commenda with the new form as seen in the *Commandite par actions*.

It is impossible in a short survey of the history and development of commercial law in medieval times to trace even briefly the history of every one of the manifold contracts of a mercantile character; but the history of insurance, owing to its intrinsic importance and to the fact that it took its present shape and form in medieval times and may be fairly regarded not as a creation of the legislature but of the merchants and traders themselves, would seem to claim especial reference.

As a special contract insurance dated only from the opening years of the 14th century. But long before that time an indirect secondary form of insurance was in common use in the trading countries of Europe. In sea loans, in contracts of commenda, for example, it is extremely common to find the risk made the object of a special clause, by which the contracting party who received the goods either expressly took over risks by land or sea, and became responsible for the safe delivery of the goods—salvi in terra—or expressly disclaimed all responsibility for the goods in case of misadventure.—Ad tuum resegum—ad risicum et fortunam Dei, maris et gentium—sana eunte nave—are the most usual forms of the clauses[1] by which the intention of the parties was declared. A passage in the oldest law treatise of the crusading kingdoms of the East, the "Livre des assises de la cour des bourgeois," shows that the use and legal signification of these clauses

[1] For these clauses see very numerous references and the treatment of the subject by Goldschmidt, p. 349 and following pages.

were well established as early as the 12th century.
"If it happen," declares the treatise[1], "that a man
entrust to another man his property to carry over
sea for gain 'en aventure de mer et des gens,' and
pirates happen to fall in with them and carry off all
that he is carrying, or the weather is bad and wrecks
the vessel and all is lost, reason commands that he
is quit in all, and that he need make no amends.
And if he has received the merchandise of good folk
to carry it 'sauf en terre,' he is bound by the law
and by the Assize to make amends according to
what he may have lost." Both clauses were in
common use, and merchants and capitalists began
to regulate the profit or commission according as
they assumed the risk or not. From a 14th century
(1335—1343) treatise on commerce, Pegolotti's
"Practica della Mercatura," it is evident that according as Florentine bills on England contained one
or other of these clauses the banker received a
commission of 10 "sous" per 100 marks or of only 20
"little sous[2]." Such differences in commission or in
share of profit were really premiums paid for the
risk undertaken, and it was but a natural result
that merchants began to make special contracts of

[1] *Le Livre des Assises des Bourgeois*, cap. 48, quoted in French
Translation of Bensa, p. 1. " S'il avient que un home baille à un
autre home de son aver à porter sur mer, à gaaing en aventure de
mer et des gens, et il avient que corsaus l'encontrent et li tolent
tout can que il porte, o il fait mauvais tens, et brise le vaisseau et
pert tout, la raison commande qu'il en est atant quite et il ne li en
deit riens amender. Et c'il avint que il resut l'aveir des bones
gens à porter sauf en terre, il est tenue de l'amender comment
qu'il seit puis perdus, par dreit et par l'asize."

[2] Bensa, *Il Contratto di Assicurazione*, pp. 31—2.

insurance. This there is every reason to believe they began to do in the opening years of the 14th century; for the earliest evidence goes back no further, and the absence of all reference to insurance in the vast mass of 13th century commercial documents of Marseilles and of the East makes it extremely probable that insurance had not developed into a special contract until the commencement of the 14th century. A clause in the statutes of the Calimala Gild of Florence of the year 1301[1] may or may not refer to special contracts of insurance, but that such contracts were in use in 1319 is proved by the books for that year of the great Florentine house of Del Bene. The entries in the books of this firm show that it paid to the Bardi, who acted as the forwarding agents of the firm, special sums for insurance[2]. For 1329 a receipt has been preserved in which the payment of 272 golden florins is acknowledged "in pagamento de risico et securitate facta per dictum dominum Gaspalem supradicto Nicolao Guicciardini pro supradictis mercantiis[3]." The documents show[4] that at this time the freight and insurance were contracted for simultaneously with the owners of the

---

[1] St. Calimalae (1301), Lb. ii. c. 4, p. 93. " Si vero aliqui mercatores euntes extra Florentiam vel morantes fecerint inter se pacta vel ordinamenta de aliquo rischio de avere quod portaverint, consules compellant tam ipsos viatores quam eorum sotios et magistros ea efficaciter observare." Quoted by Goldschmidt, p. 359, note 78.

[2] Bensa, *Il Contratto di Assicurazione*, pp. 51—53. Document i. p. 184.

[3] Bensa, *op. cit.*, p. 53. [4] *Op. cit.*

ship in which the goods were to be conveyed.
Shippers were the first insurers. The earliest
contract of insurance which has been preserved
dates from the year 1347 and is interesting as
showing the care taken to avoid all suspicion of
usury. The insurer feigns to have received a loan
"gratis et amore" of the sum of money for which the
insurance was effected and promises faithfully to
return it, unless the ship arrives safe and sound
in port[1]. The contract of insurance had freed itself

[1] A.D. 1347. Brought to light by Bensa, Document iii. p. 192.
"In nomine D. Amen. Ego Georgius Lecavellum civis Janue
confiteor tibi Bartholomeo Basso filio Bartholomei me habuisse et
recepisse a te *mutuo gratis et amore* libras centum septem Janue.
Renuncians exceptioni dicte pecunie ex dicta causa non *habite*,
non *recepte*, non *numerate* et omni juri.

Quas libras centum septem Janue, vel totidem ejusdem monete
pro ipsis, convenio et promitto tibi solemni stipulationi reddere et
restituere tibi aut tuo certo nuntio per me vel meum nuncium.

Usque ad menses sex proxime venturos, *salvo et reservato, et
hoc sane intellecto, quod si cocha* tua de duabus copertis et uno
timono, vocata S. Clara que nunc est in portu Janue parata, Deo
dante, ire et navigare presentialiter ad Majorichas, *iverit et
navigaverit recto viagio* de portu Janue navigando usque ad
Majorichas et *ibi applicuerit sana et salva, quod tunc* et eo casu
sit praesens instrumentum cassum et *nullius valoris* ut si facta (sic)
non fuisset. Suscipiens in me omnem risicum et periculum dicte
quantitatis pecunie quousque dicta cocha applicuerit Majoricis,
navigante recto viagio ut supra. Et etiam si dicta cocha fuerit
sana et salva in aliqua parte, usque ad dictos sex menses, sit
similiter praesens instrumentum cassum et nullius valoris ac si
factum non fuisset. Et similiter si dicta cocha mutaverit
viagium sit dictum instrumentum cassum et nullius valoris ac si
factum non fuisset.

In dictum modum et sub dictis conditionibus promitto tibi
dictam solutionem facere, alioquin penam dupli dicte quantitatis
pecunie tibi stipulanti dare et solvere promitto cum restitutione

from its connection with the contract for the freight
and had assumed the form of a feigned loan. For
some 20 years it continues in the documents to
retain this form, but from 1368 onwards it begins to
take the guise of a feigned sale[1] "nomine venditionis

damnorum et expensarum que propterea fierent vel sustinerentur
litis vel extra, ratis manentibus supradictis sub ypotheca et
obligatione bonorum meorum, habitorum vel habendorum.

Actum Janue in Banchis in angulo domus Carli et Bonifaci
Ususmaris fratrum, anno dom. nat. mcccxxxxvii. indit. xv.
secundum cursum Janue, die xxiii Octobris circa vesperas. Testes
Nicolaus de Tacio draperius et Johannes de Rechio filius Bonanati
cives Janue."

[1] Bensa, Document 8, p. 200.   Contract of Reinsurance for
July 12, 1370.   "Nos Griffedus Benavia et Martinus Maruffus
cives Janue confitemur tibi Bartholomeo Lomellino civi Janue q.
Surleonis Nos a te *emisse*, habuisse et recepisse tot de tuis rebus et
mercibus—Renunciantes......

... dare et solvere libras centum viginti quinque Janue hinc ad
menses sex proxime venturos...

Salvo et specialiter reservato, si illa quantitas quarumcunque
rerum et mercium, ad rixicum cujus Jullianus Grillus se obligavit
Johanni Sacho sub certa reservatione, juxta formam publici instru-
menti, scripti manu publici notarii, et que onerata fuit in cocha
patronizata per Bartholeum Verme de Saulo, vel alium pro eo, in
portu Clusarum de Flandria, sana et salva conducta et exornata
fuerit, tunc et eo casu praesens instrumentum sit cassum et nullius
valoris et pro rato.

Et risicum hujusmodi inceptum esse intelligatur quum dicta
cocha in Cadese primo applicuit."

(In margine) : Eundo Clusas recto viagio, possit capere ubicunque. Non teneamur de aliquo tributo dato seu soluto in Cadese
alicui.

Cf. Bensa, No. 9 and Contract of Insurance for 1425, Bensa,
no. 16, p. 223 : "Confessi fuerunt sese emisse, habuisse et
recepisse tot de ipsius Antonii rebus et mercibus causa infra-
scripta...salvo et specialiter reservato etc...." and no. 19 (1427
A.D.), p. 228.

M.   10

et cambii." From the first it was required that the person in whose favour the contract of insurance was made should have a real interest in the safe arrival. Insurance was not considered as a mere wager dependent on the safe arrival of the ship, but was a true contract of indemnity. For instance, in a contract of insurance (1370) made on behalf of a certain Rapallo, the insurer promised that Rapallo's right should not be prejudiced by the fact that he has no share in the ship, which implies that the contract, without this special clause, might have been invalidated by this circumstance. In course of time however the clause—"habeat vel non habeat, participet vel non participet" or more briefly, "habeat vel non"—were introduced in the contracts of insurance, and finally this clause was always included. It is not probable however that this clause made it a matter of indifference whether the insured had a real interest in the safe arrival of the ship or not, for very often it was stated that, while the insured had no interest in the particular goods insured, he contracted the insurance to safeguard other interests:—"protestans quod in praedictis non participat, sed haec fieri facit pro sua electione, cautela, cautione, et juvimento[1]." The two clauses would seem to

---

[1] Bensa, p. 66. "Non è però a credere che questa clausola importasse esenzione assoluta dell' assicurato da ogni necessità d' interesse al salvo arrivo della nave, ma piuttosto che fosse diretta a ribadire il concetto che qualunque sorte d' interesse potesse legittimamente coprirsi colla difesa dell' assicurazione. Se così non fosse, non avrebbe spiegazione la clausola, bene spesso apposto nei contratti. 'Protestans quod in praedictis non par-

show that an interest of some kind was necessary and that an insurance which was a mere wager was not allowable. In the early documents ship or goods alone or ship and goods together were objects of insurance. When it was goods that were insured, the ship in which they were to be transported was clearly indicated. Insurances of goods to be conveyed in an unnamed ship—in quovis—were rare even in fairly late times, but even as early as the middle of the 14th century there was a special case in which the ship was left uncertain. When goods had to be transhipped at an intermediate port, the choice of the fresh ship was sometimes at least left to the insured[1]. In the Genoan documents the limits of the time within which the insurer was responsible for the risk were carefully fixed. In the case of the cargo the risk began from the moment the ship set sail, and was terminated when the goods were

ticipat, sed haec fieri facit pro sua electione, cautela, cautione, et jhuvimento." Goldschmidt, pp. 370—1, note 114, opposes this view. "Vielmehr wollen sie (i.e. the clauses) augenscheinlich dem Versicherten den Nachweis des Interesses überhaupt ersparen; ja sie lassen die Deutung zu, dass sogar den Nachweis des mangelnden Interesses ausgeschlossen sei." Legislation however, Goldschmidt adds, soon declared against such contracts. "Jedenfalls ist die Gesetzgebung bald dagegen eingeschritten, sei es, dass dergleichen Verträge nur mit Erlaubnis der Regierung gestattet wurden ; sei es, schlechthin untersagt."

[1] Bensa, p. 66, and document 6, p. 197 (1350 A.D.). For an insurance "in quovis" with no ship specified, see Bensa, No. 24, p. 236 "...Super illa navi patronizata per *quamvis* personam quam ascendet et veniet dictus Nicolaus Andreas Cibo..." A.D. 1433.

Bensa, p. 70, refers to Straccha who discusses this clause and who declares that it was common in English policies.

disembarked[1] in port. For the ship, on the other hand, the insurance held good until the ship had reached its port of destination safe and sound and had remained there 24 hours[2]. That property already lost at the time of the contract of insurance, but the loss of which was unknown at the time, could be legally insured is shown by the fact that in contracts where the insurance was effected not for a definite voyage but, as was occasionally the case, for a definite time, which however did not usually amount to more than a year, the risk was sometimes declared to run before the date of the contract. Change of route from the first freed the insurers from all risk. The clauses in the early documents, borrowed from

[1] V. Bensa, p. 70, e.g. Insurance of Merchandise in ship to sail from Aigues-Mortes to Ephesus and Rhodes. Bensa, Document 13, p. 216. "Salvo et specialiter reservato, si illa quantitas rerum bonorum et mercium...*conducta* et EXONERATA fuerit *in ipsis locis* Teologi et Roddi, vel altero eorum, ad salvamentum, *tunc* et eo casu praesens instrumentum sit cassum etc....et intelligatur inceptum hujusmodi rixicum, cum dicta navis recesserit et velificaverit de Aquis mortuis, et stet et duret, eundo, stando, navigando, onerando, et exonerando patronus, de dicto loco Aquarum mortuarum usque ad dicta loca Teologi et Roddi, quomodocumque et qualitercunque voluerit, quousque dicta quantitas rerum, bonorum et mercium *conducta* et EXONERATA fuerit in Teologo et Roddo, vel in altero ipsorum duorum locorum ad salvamentum." No. 14, p. 218; insurance on goods from Montrone to Aigues-Mortes. "E quando la detta roba sarà *posta* e SCARICA in terra a salvamento in Aqua Morta che in quello caso i detti assicuratori siano liberi e disobbligati della sicurtà per loro fatta."

[2] v. Bensa, p. 70, and Document, p. 213. Insurance of a galley, 1394. "Salvo et specialiter reservato, si quedam galeacia" etc...."applicuerit in dicto portu Janue ad salvamentum et ibi steterit per xxiiii horas, *tunc* et eo casu" etc. Also no. 16 (A.D. 1425), p. 223.

the contracts of sea loan—recto viagio, eundo et redeundo, recto et continuato viagio—were short and strict, but by the end of the 14th century a clause had been elaborated which is substantially the same as that in use in modern times and which, while allowing all reasonable freedom of action, insists that the destination shall not be changed:—
" eundo, stando, navigando, onerando, exonerando patronus a dextris et a sinistris, per rectum et indirectum, antecedendo retrocedendo, quocunque ubicunque, quomodocumque et qualitercumque voluerit patronus vel alius pro eo, *viagio tamen non mutato*[1]." The "consilia" of the jurist Bosco (1399—1435) show that by common usage the insurers were not held responsible for losses caused by barratry on the part of the captain. " I confess," he writes, " that by the common and unwritten custom of the country, and by the general and tacit understanding of those concluding the contracts, there is one exceptional case in which the risk pertains to the insured, to wit when it is proved that the things were lost of set purpose by the fraud and contrivance of the captain[2]."

The Genoan contracts do not specify in detail the dangers against which the insurance is effected, and Bosco argued that the insurance applied to all misadventures " usual or unusual." In Pisan and

---

[1] Bensa, p. 71, who refers to Straccha's 17th century treatise on insurance. The clause is found almost verbatim in an insurance upon a ship for the year 1425. Bensa, no. 16, p. 224.

[2] Bensa, 74, and for Bosco, French Translation of Bensa, p. 29, note 2.

Florentine contracts, on the other hand, the enumeration is so complete and detailed as to leave little loop-hole for evasion on the part of the insurers. The risks which the insurers run, declares a Florentine contract of insurance for the year 1397, are " of God, the sea, of nations, fire, jettisons, restrain by Lords or by communes or any other person, of letter of marque, of arrest and of every other case, peril, fortune, impediment or mishap which in any way could occur or might have occurred, no matter how or under what condition the cases might occur, excepted only what concerns custom dues and ballast[1]." It was not unusual in the contract for insurers especially to except certain risks for which they did not wish to be held liable, and general average was often thus excepted by a not uncommon clause : " non teneantur de devastato corpore navis ad salvamentum tunc existentis[2]." The premium was paid in advance, and this was almost inevitable in the earlier stages of the contract when insurance assumed the form of a feigned sale. With such a form of contract the insurer would have no legal remedy against his debtor for the premium. Later on the custom of prepayment of the premium was in several places enforced by the law.

---

[1] Bensa, Document 14, pp. 217—8. A.D. 1397. "E il rischio che gli assicuratori corrono in sulla detta roba... ; si è di Dio, di mare, di gente, di fuoco, di gitto di mare, di ritinemento di signori o di comuni, o d' alcun altra persona, o di rappresaglie o d' arresto e d' ogni altro caso, pericolo, fortuna, impedimento o caso sinistro, che per verun modo ne potese intervenire o fusse intervenuto, e fussono fatti i casi come si volessero o di che condizione, salvo di stiva o di dugana."   [2] Bensa, p. 76.

Originating in the early years of the 14th century as a separate contract, insurance developed rapidly and by the close of the century was, in Italy at any rate, a common form of contract. In 1393 a single Genoan notary within 3 weeks drew up no less than 80 contracts of insurance[1], and the consilia of Bosco (1399–1435) which have in recent times been rediscovered by Bensa bear out this view and declare that a contract insurance was "no unusual thing," but "such as many merchants of Genoa make, of whom some have no other mode of livelihood than this[2]." The law and customs of insurance are in their main outlines the outcome of the usage of merchants as expressed in the written contracts of insurance.

The clauses of these contracts by the 15th century had broadly speaking taken the form and substance that for centuries and even in modern times they were to retain. Legislation was to declare and sometimes to modify the law, and judicial decisions were to recognise fresh usages as they gradually arose, and to give precision and a fixed signification to the clauses that substantially unaltered were repeated from century to century in contracts of insurance, but the clauses of the early contracts remain the basis of the modern law of insurance of the civilised

[1] Bensa, p. 79.

[2] Bensa, p. 79, quotes Bosco: "Marcus propter lucrari fecit plures assecûrationes sicut faciunt plurimi mercatores de Janua quorum aliqui de nullo alio vivunt quam de hujusmodi quaestu, qui quandoque est utilissimus, quandoque damnòsus, secundum cursum temporum et fortunae blandimenta vel adversiones. Unde Marcus non facit rem insolitam sed rem usitatam et consuetam fieri in Bancis a plurimis, etiam ex sapientioribus."

world. Policies of marine insurance are to this day made in a form which on the face of it is clumsy, imperfect, and obscure. But the effect of every clause and almost every word has been settled by a series of decisions, and the common form really implies a whole body of judicial rules, " which originated either in decisions of the courts upon the construction or on the mode of applying the policy, or in customs proved before the court so clearly or so often as to have been long recognised by the courts without further proof. Since those decisions and the recognition of those customs, merchants and underwriters have for many years continued to enter into policies in the same form. According to ordinary principle, then, the later policies must be held to have been entered into upon the basis of those decisions and customs. If so, the rules determined by those decisions are part of the contract[1]." Upon the framework of the old contract of insurance elaborated in Italy during the closing centuries of the Middle Ages and transferred by international trade to the other commercial countries of Europe, a vast and complex body of Law has been reared. To a certain extent it is new wine in old bottles. The modern law of insurance is more complicated and far more precise than the law and custom of the 14th or 15th centuries, but the development from the old to the new has been slow and natural, and the old and the new alike have the same underlying general principles. The development of the legal rules and

[1] 3 Q. B. Div. 558, 562, quoted by Pollock, *Contracts*, pp. 258—9.

principles of insurance has in reality been effected
by the natural development in the usages of the
merchant class, and judicial decisions and legislation
have everywhere done little but recognise and enforce
those usages and check those particular forms of
insurance that were liable to grave abuse. Thus the
early laws of Genoa and Barcelona forbid insurances
to the full value of the cargo. A Genoan law passed
about 1420 only allowed insurances to the amount of
half the value of the ship including the value of the
equipment, though an earlier statute had permitted
insurance of two-thirds of the value[1]. In Barcelona
the regulations of 1435 only allowed insurances on
goods in native ships to be effected to three-fourths
of the value and declared that any excess of this
amount should not be recoverable by the insured,
though the insurers were entitled to retain the full
premium paid : if loaded on board foreign ships
however the goods could only be insured to the
extent of half their value[2]. Modified in 1436 and
1458 this rule received (1484) the form that it long
retained in the important regulations of Barcelona
on insurance, which were translated into various
languages and exercised a considerable influence
upon the law of insurance by giving precision to the

[1] Bensa, Document VI. p. 159. "Participibus vero vasorum et
navigiorum liceat assecurari se facere usque ad medietatem
valoris et pretii, vel estimationis dictorum vasorum et navigiorum,
computato etiam armamento ipsorum": for earlier statute, Bensa,
p. 89, and note 1.

[2] Pardessus, *Collection des Lois Maritimes*, vol. v. pp. 496—7,
Regulations of 1435, c. 3. For case of foreign ships, cap. 4, pp.
495—6.

usages and promoting uniformity in the laws of the chief countries of Europe. " The councillors and prudhommes ordain," declares the first chapter of these regulations, " that all ships and other vessels of our Lord the King, and those of foreigners of whatever nation they may be,......and all goods loaded and transported by them to any part of the world, to whomever it may belong whether subjects of our Lord the King or foreigners, may be insured at Barcelona, to wit those of the subjects of our Lord the King for seven-eighths, and those of strangers for three quarters of the real price which the things insured shall have cost, in which price shall be reckoned the expenses of the expeditions, the cost of the insurances, and other expenses[1]."

In Italy the earliest regulations absolutely forbade all insurances in favour of foreigners, but a more enlightened policy prevailed and the restrictions fell into desuetude, and during the course of the 15th century full liberty of insurance was conceded at Genoa to foreigners except for voyages between the various ports of the Mediterranean and of the Black Sea. In Barcelona the various regulations issued during the same period mark an advance in the same direction. The earliest law of 1435 did not allow the insurance of foreign goods in foreign vessels, while the regulations of 1484 simply limit the amount of the insurance.

In both Italy and Barcelona legislation during the 15th century declared contracts of insurance invalid when the loss of the property insured was

[1] Pardessus, *op. cit.*, vol. v. p. 524.

known or might reasonably be supposed to be known at the time the contract was signed[1], and the Barcelona statute of 1484 "to remove all incertitude as to the time when the news may have been known" allowed for every league that the news had to travel by land an hour from the time that the news first reached dry land. The early Spanish and Italian legislation also settled the question of jurisdiction in cases relating to insurance, and both alike conferred it upon the commercial courts[2]. On the whole however the early legislation did but regulate existing usage, and the immediate origin of the principles of insurance lies in customs and contracts of the medieval merchants of Italy.

[1] Bensa, for Italy, p. 89. For Barcelona, Pardessus, v. p. 514 (St. 1458, cap. 14), pp. 536—7 (St. 1484, cap. 17). For other city regulations see Goldschmidt, p. 379, n. 137.

[2] Bensa, Document 3, p. 153. "De his autem praemissis cautionibus et securationibus que fierent inter cives seu districtuales Florentie et pro mercantiis et rebus eorum vel alicujus eorum, possit et debeat per *dictum officium* (*i.e.* of the Mercanzia) cognosci procedi, jus fieri et terminari...et tales securationes... debeant observari et executioni mandari simpliciter et secundum bonam fidem et *consuetudinem mercatorum*." Pardessus, v. p. 513, note 1; p. 512, St. 1458, cap. 9. "Aucun assuré ne pourra decliner la competence ou juridiction de la dite cour du consulat, ni porter des affaires ailleurs qu'a ladite cour."

CONCLUSION.

THE whole history of Law Merchant in Europe during the Middle Ages was characterised by a constant advance towards uniformity and by the successful assertion of new principles of law. It was developed in local courts, in which directly or indirectly the merchants declared the law. The merchants of the fair courts of St Ives, or the merchants and mariners of Barcelona, were alike the "doomsmen" of the court; it was the function of the judge merely to proclaim and execute the judgment of the merchants. In Italy the judges occupied a more important position; but here again they were wholly or in part taken from among the merchants, as was the case in the later commercial courts of France and Germany. The international nature of trade even in medieval times, the general similarity in economic conditions that gradually arose, and the predominant influence of the legal conceptions and the commercial usages of the Italian merchants, all combined to make the law administered by merchants to merchants more uniform and international in character. It is however difficult to draw a hard and fast line separating the Early Law Merchant from the Modern. All dividing lines in the history of human institutions are to a certain extent arbitrary and artificial. Still in the 16th century the Law Merchant entered upon a new stage of its development, and its early history may fairly be regarded as closed. All the great principles that mark the commercial law of modern times had then been evolved and success-fully asserted, and different forces and influences were becoming important in determining its future history and development. The age of the great writers on mercantile law, of Marquardus, Straccha and Malynes, was dawning. Legislation, not so much of single cities, as in the earlier period, but of great and powerful kingdoms with definite commercial policies of their own, began freely to declare and to modify the law. The period of formation when the Law Merchant had to indicate important principles opposed to the principles alike of Roman and Germanic law was passed, and the early history of the law, the history of the creation and successful assertion of its leading maxims in the local courts of fair or town or staple, ended, as so much of medieval history ended, in the 16th century. By that time every great country in Europe had recognised in commercial cases the principles of representation, the negotiability of bills of exchange, the liability of the real property of the debtor for his debts, the validity, to a certain extent at least, of formless contracts, the necessity of speedy justice, the importance of the principles of equity and the claims of the bona fide possessor to the protection of the law. The legal relations of partners to one another and to the outside world had, in almost every important point, been definitely settled, and a new commercial contract, insurance, had been evolved and the legal principles that were to govern its development clearly marked. The medieval merchant had laboured, and the modern world had entered into his labours.

Both Canon and Roman law exercised an influence upon the development of the Law Merchant. Canon law recognised the principle of representation[1], laid stress upon equity and good faith and on the binding force of a simple promise, and exerted a favourable influence on the growth of summary methods of procedure. So far its influence was on the side of the Law Merchant. On the other hand the prohibition of usury by the Church cramped and hindered trade, and so far as it was effective simply served to raise the rate of interest. But the importance of the laws against usury has often been greatly exaggerated. When necessary, the merchant rarely failed to find expedients to evade them and did not hesitate upon occasion to defy them. At Genoa, for example, any attempt to make use of the Canon law on usury in order to invalidate contracts of insurance was strictly forbidden and punished. Moreover the Church itself gradually relaxed the rigour of the law; the canonists began to recognise the right of the lender to compensation for "damnum emergens" and "lucrum cessans" and "the total result was that any merchant or indeed any person in a trading centre where there

[1] C. 68, 72, de reg. juris, in vi. (5.12), referred to by Gold-schmidt, p. 276, note 139.

were opportunities of business investments (outside
money lending itself), could with a perfectly clear
conscience and without fear of molestation contract
to receive periodical interest from a person to whom
be lent money; provided only that he first lent it to
him gratuitously for a period which might be made
very short, so that technically the payment would
not be reward for the use, but compensation for non-
return of the money[1]." On the whole the doctrines
and principles of the Canon law told in favour of
the Law Merchant. On several important principles
the two systems of law were in substantial and
permanent agreement, while the prohibition of usury
by the Church was not difficult to evade and, as
opportunities for the employment of capital increased
with the general expansion of trade, that prohibition
was gradually relaxed.

Roman law had a vastly greater influence than
Canon law upon the Law Merchant in Western
Europe. Numerous rules of Roman law found their
way into the great Sea Code of Barcelona; and in
spite of bitter complaints the English Admiralty
continued to make use of the "Law Civil." At Como
and Pera, Piacenza and Cremona, Bologna and
Florence the special mercantile statutes expressly
refer to the Roman law as a subsidiary source to be
used where the statutes gave no rule[2]. The vast
mass of early commercial documents of the lands
of the Mediterranean and the fair bonds of the

[1] W. Ashley, *Economic History*, vol. I. part ii. p. 402.
[2] Lattes, *Il Diritto Commerciale nelle città Italiane*, p. 72, and
p. 76, note 11.

Netherlands are drawn up in the technical language of the Roman lawyer. It is true that perhaps the most striking feature of these early commercial contracts is the almost invariable renunciation by the contracting parties of many of the "exceptions" and rules of Roman law; but this very renunciation would seem to imply that in the absence of express renunciation the principles of Roman law were applicable.

Roman law was, in the main, the basis of commercial contracts and consequently, in the main, the basis of the Law Merchant. "It is a most notable fact, but not on that account less important," writes Lattes in a work in which the mercantile statutes of the medieval cities of Italy have been examined and analysed with scrupulous care and thoroughness, "that in the theory of obligations, the Roman laws, preserving an authority much greater than in any other part of the law, were applied, transcribed and imitated, so as to form the basis of modern codes, with the few modifications imposed in recent times. To the modifications the mercantile statutes contributed much....But *these statutes themselves...in reality only contain* a few *fragmentary dispositions and* a few *remarkable exceptions to the principles of Roman law*[1]." "The contract of affreightment, the doctrine of general average, and the contract of bottomry" are all covered by the principles of Roman law[2].

[1] Lattes, *op. cit.* p. 122.
[2] Carter, *English Legal Institutions*, p. 263. Cf. Goldschmidt, 78, and note 93.

But great as was the influence of Roman law, the customs and usages of the merchant himself remained the decisive factor in the development of the Law Merchant. When the true interests of commerce were at stake the merchant persistently and obstinately refused to recognise the rules of Roman law. The principle of representation was carried in the Law Merchant far further than ever Roman law carried it; the honest purchaser was protected, and formless contract recognised, to a large extent, as binding. The Law Merchant no doubt rested upon a solid basis of Roman law, and in later times as commerce with the discovery of the new world and the growth of capital became more world-wide and approximated more closely to the commercial relations of the vast Roman Empire, direct borrowing from Roman law became perhaps more open and more extensive. Even in England Lord Holt and Lord Mansfield introduced whole branches of the civil law[1]. But in medieval times the merchant in the long run rejected or accepted, extended or restricted, the principles of the Roman law as the interests of commerce required. In no small measure Roman law was the raw material of the Law Merchant, but that material the medieval merchant fashioned and framed as seemed good to him. "Out of his own needs and his own views" the merchant of the Middle Ages created the Law Merchant.

---

[1] Smith, *Commercial Law*, Historical Introduction.

APPENDIX I.

Willelmus de Temesford queritur de Augustino Capello de Temesford, quod Idem Augustinus iniuste ei detinet et non solvit III. quarteria frumenti, que de eo mutuavit die Jovis proxima post Invencionem Sancte Crucis anno regni regis Edwardi XVI°., et unum quarterium siliginis et unum quarterium brasii que similiter eidem Augustino tradidit per particulas prout indiguit: precium tocius bladi XXXII. solidorum. Quod quidem bladum debuit ei solvisse ad festum Sancti Michaelis proximum sequens, unde Idem A. nichil hactenus ei persolvit, set totum detinuit et adhuc detinet ad dampnum suum. Predictus Augustinus presens dicit se non fuisse attachiatum per quod attachiamentum respondere debuit, et consideratum fuit quod respondisset ad incopamentum dicti Willelmi: qui quidem Augustinus respondere noluit, set in contemptu tocius Curie recessit. Quare considerandum fuit, quod dictus Willelmus a prefato Augustino tanquam de indefenso recuperaret debitum suum unacum dampnis suis, et quod predictus Augustinus pro iniusta detentione fuisset in misericordia, plegius i equs. Et super hoc venit quidem Walterus Daneys et optulit se probaturum dictum equm esse suum et ad hoc petiit admitti cum probacione sua, cui responsum fuit ex parte adversa, quod fraudulenter optulit se probaturum alienum catallum. Et quia idem Walterus in calumpnia sua tenebatur pro suspecto eo quod inhonesta persona fuit nec habuit tantum in catallis et quod ipse per fraudem et collusionem hoc fecerat, consideratum fuit quod inde rei veritas per bonam inquisicionem inquireretur, utrum dictus equs erat suus tempore attachiamenti vel non. Et super hoc electa fuit inquisicio. Que venit et dicit per sacramentum suum quod dictus Walterus Daneys equm predictum arravit per argentum Dei de prefato Augustino in villa de Temesford die dominica proxima ante attachiamentum factum ; quod quidem attachiamentum suum erat die Martis sequenti, set in decepcione dicti Willelmi de Temesford et per collusionem, ut idem Willelmus elongaretur de catallis suis ; et ponitur in respectum judicium donec per mercatores melius discuciatur. Et convocatis mercatoribus de diversis communitatibus et aliis in plena Curia, consideratum est quod dictus Walterus Daneys, ex quo nunquam posuit se in Inquisicione predicta que quidem Inquisicio capta erat adtunc tanquam ex officio senescalli et ex quo Idem W. per argentum dei collatum prefato Augustino empcionem equi predicti secundum legem mercatoriam sufficienter confirmavit, quod idem Walterus veniat cum tercia manu sua de bonis hominibus electis et fide dignis ad probandum dictum equm esse suum, ita quod dictus Augustinus tempore attachiamenti in eodem equo artem habuit neque partem. Qui quidem Walterus venit et sufficienter fecit legem. Ideo idem W. inde quietus cum equo predicto et prefatus Willelmus pro falso clamore in misericordia et condonatur.

APPENDIX II.

Curia de Mercurii proxima post festum sancti
Dunstani Nicholaus Legge queritur de Nicholao de
Myldenhal quod iniuste eum impedit quod partem
habere non potest de quodam bove quem Nicholaus de
Myldenhal emerat in presencia sua in villa sancti Ivonis
die lune ultimo preterito secundum usum Mercatorum ad
dampnum suum duorum solidorum, desicut promptus
erat solveré medietatem peccunie cuius tota summa
continebat viis. vid.

Et predictus Nicholaus defendit verba Curie et dicit
quod lex mercatorum bene permittit quod quilibet
Mercator participet de mercandisa carnificum si partem
inde in tempore vendicionis calumpniaverit, set quod
ipse Nicholaus Legge non fuit presens tempore empcionis
nec partem calumpniavit promptus est facere quod Curia
considerat. Et Nicholaus Legge dicit quod prefatus
Nicholaus de Mildenale ad legem venire non debet eo
quod incopatus fuit quod debuit ei negasse habere
partem bovis predicti, quod quidem verbum non defendebat. Quare Idem N. Legge petit judicium de ipso
sicut de indefenso. Unde consideratum est quod dictus
N. Legge recuperet versus ipsum is. pro dampnis suis.
Et Idem N. de Mildenale in misericordia iis., plegius
Johannes de Thoref.

APPENDIX III.

Willelmus de Pappeworth queritur de Johanne de
Kent quod idem Johannes iniuste ei detinet viginti tres
solidos et quatuor denarios de uno equo vendito eidem
Johanni pro xliii*s*. iv*d*. et pro uno quadrante ei
tradito ad argentum dei die Mercurii proximo preterito
in Curia Willelmi Manger apud sanctum Ivonem ; quos
quidem denarios idem Johannes debuit solvisse incon-
tinenti eidem : de quibus non solvit nisi tantum xxiii*s*.
iv*d*. et totum residuum scil. xx*s*. retinuit et adhuc
detinet ad dampnum ipsius Willelmi dimidium Marce et
ducit sectam.

Et predictus Johannes presens defendit verba que
fuerant defendenda et dicit expresse se in nichillo ei
teneri et quod ita sit promptus est ad verificandum per
Legem suam si Curia consideraverit.

Et predictus Willelmus dicit quod ad legem venire
non debet racione quod incopavit ipsum Johannem fuisse
seysitum de i quadranti eidem tradito nomine argenti
Dei quod quidem argentum Dei idem Johannes non
defendit et insuper petit iudicium et consideracionem
mercatorum si predictus Johannes per legem suam
adnichilare possit accionem et demandam ipsius Willelmi

necve.   Et ponitur judicium in respectum propter
tenuitatem curie usque diem Mercurii.   Ad quem diem
consideratum fuit per Mercatores quod, ex quo contractus
factus inter dictum W. querentem et prefatum J.
defendentem affirmatus fuit per quadrantem datum
predicto Willelmo in argentum Dei, quod quidem
argentum Dei dictus J. non defendebat, remaneret
tanquam indefensus.   Et dictus W. reciperet etc. et
Johannes in misericordia II s.   Solvit, et taxata sunt
dampna ad II s.

APPENDIX IV.

Vitalis de Grafham conquerens optulit se per Robertum de Grafham attornatum suum versus Hugonem Pope super iniusta detentione. Et testatur quod dictus Hugo districtus fuit per unum equm, qui est in Curia Abbatis, die lune proxima post festum sancti Dunstani ultimo. Et super hoc venit quidam Alanus de Berkhamsted die martis proxima sequenti et allegavit in plena Curia dictum equm esse suum et quod ipse illum equm emerat ad opus suum proprium de quodam Thoma de Rammesden, et quod ita sit voluntate sua spontanea posuit se in Inquisicione et pars adversa similiter. Et inquisicio scilicet Ricardus Scot Radulphus Scot Adam faber Absalom Sterne Johannes de Waltham Walterus ...veniunt et dicunt per sacramentum quod dictus Alanus iniuste calumpniat equm predictum tanquam suum nec habet partem in eodem quia Idem Alanus ad opus predicti Hugonis eundem equm emit tanquam valettus et abrokator eiusdem Hugonis et quod idem Hugo mandavit ei...London quod solueret nomine eiusdem Hugonis viginti solidos pro eodem equo ; quos quidem denarios idem Alanus mutuo recepit predicto die lune de Radulpho de Honcton de sancto Ivone ; et hoc ex recognicione dicti Radulphi. Quare consideratum est quod predictus equs teneatur et capiatur plus donec dictus Hugo justificaverit se ad respondendum predicto Vitali vel suo attornato et apreciatus est equs per Willelmum de Hocton Nicholaum Legge Thomam de...et Johannem Pake Juratos ad ii Marcas. Et datus dies predicto atornato usque in crastinum apostolorum Philippi et Jacobi in proximis Nundinis futuris.

APPENDIX V.

Alicia uxor Nicholai le Tanur queritur de Matilda Ffraunceys; plegii de prosequendo Nicholaus Tannator et Mauritius Sutor; plegii defendentes vir eius et Hugo Bacun. Et partes optulerunt se et Alicia dicit se nolle prosequi versus prefatam Matildam super tres busselos brasii inventos in manibus predicte Matilde pro quibus ipsa ad querelam dicte Alicie fuit attachiata. Ideo ipsa Alicia et plegii sui scilicet Nicholaus le Tanur et Mauritius Sutor pro non secta sua adiudicata est ad Carcerem et de Carcere fecit finem per xii*d*.

Et super hoc senescallus ex officio suo tanquam pro secta domini Regis petiit a dicta Matilda Ffraunceys in cuius seysina dictum brasium fuit inventum qualiter se defendere voluerit quod brasium predictum furtive non fuerat perquisitum. Que dicit quod de bono et malo ponit se in Deo et in vicinis juratis; qui veniunt et dicunt per sacramentum suum quod quidam extraneus de quo ipsa Matilda non habuit noticiam dictum brasium portavit ad domum ipsius Matilde; super quod brasium ipsa Matilda ad instantiam dicti extranei tradidit ei ex mutuo VIII denarios nec habuit ipsum extraneum suspectum de aliquo latrocinio. Et ideo consideratum est quod dicta Matilda eat inde quieta unacum brasio suo predicto.

AUTHORITIES.

Black Book of Admiralty, ed. Travers Twiss, 1871—1876.

Britton, ed. Nichols, 1865.

Bracton, *Tractatus de Legibus*, 1569.

Little Red Book of Bristol, ed. Bickley, 1900.

Munimenta Gildhallae, ed. Riley, 1859—1862.

Records of Leicester, ed. Bateson, 1899.

Records of St Ives' Fair for the year 1275, ed. F. W. Maitland in *Select Pleas in Manorial Courts*.

Records of St Ives' Fair for the year 1291. (Augmentation Office Court Rolls, Portf. 16, No. 16.) A few cases are given in the appendices.

Select Pleas of the Court of Admiralty, ed. Marsden, 1892 —1897.

Statutes of the Realm, vol. i. 1810.

Bergamo, *Gild Statutes of* 1457, ed. 1780.

Brescia, *Gild Statutes of* 1429, ed. 1788.

Florence, *Statutes* (1301) *of Calimala Gild*, ed. Filippi, 1889.

Genoa, *Leges Genuenses*, ed. Poggi, 1901.

Mantua, *Gild Statutes of* 1400, ed. Portioli, 1887.

Pisa, *Statuti de Pisa*, ed. Bonaini, 1859—1870.

Monumenta Historiae Patriae, especially the two volumes: Chartae, Leges Municipales.

Monumenta Historico-juridica Slavorum Meridionalium.

Deutsche Rechtsquellen des Mittelalters, ed. Wasserschleben.

Hildesheim Urkundenbuch, vol. i.

Urkunden zur städtischen Verfassungsgeschichte, ed. Keutgen, 1901.

Documents relatifs à l Histoire de l'Industrie et du Commerce en France, ed. Fagniez, 1898—1900.

Documents inédits sur le commerce de Marseille au Moyen Age, ed. Blancard, 1884, 1885.

Collection de Lois Maritimes, ed. Pardessus.

Arias, *I Trattati Commerciali della Repubblica Fiorentina*, 1901.

Arias, *Studi e Documenti di Storia di Diritto*.

Bensa, *Il Contratto di Assicurazione nel Medio Evo*, 1884.

Bensa, *Histoire du Contrat d'Assurance au Moyen Age*, traduit par Valéry, 1897. This translation does not contain the documents of the Italian original.

Bonolis, *La Giurisdizione della Mercanzia in Firenze nel Secolo XIV*, 1901.

Brunner, *Deutsche Rechtsgeschichte*, vol. ii. 1892.

Brunner, *Forschungen*, 1894.

Bruschettini, *Trattato dei Titoli al Portatore*, 1898.

Carter, *English Legal Institutions*, 1902.

Cunningham, *Growth of English Industry and Commerce*, vol. i. 1896.

Del Vecchio e Casanova, *Le Rappresaglie nei Comuni Medievali*, 1894.

Desjardins, *Introduction historique à l'Étude du droit commercial maritime*, 1890.

Des Marez, *La Lettre de Foire à Ypres*, 1901.

Doren, *Untersuchungen zur Geschichte der Kaufmannsgilden des Mittelalters*, 1893.

Endemann, *Studien in der romanisch-kanonistischen Wirthschafts- und Rechtslehre*, 1874.

Freundt, *Das Wechselrecht der Postglossatoren*, 1899.

Glasson, *Les Juges et Consuls des Marchands*, 1897.

Goldschmidt, *Handbuch des Handelsrechts*, vol. i. 1891.

Goldschmidt, *Vermischte Schriften*, 1901.

Gross, *Gild Merchant*, 1890.

Hegel, *Städte und Gilden der germanischen Völker*, 1891.

Heusler, *Deutsches Privatrecht*.

Holdsworth, *History of English Law*, 1903.

Holtzendorff, *Encyklopädie der Rechtswissenschaft*, 1904.

Huvelin, *Le Droit des Marchés et des Foires*, 1897.

Huvelin, *Travaux Récents sur l'histoire de la Lettre de Change*, 1901.

Huvelin, *L'Histoire du Droit Commercial* (Conception Générale, État Actuel des Études), 1904. An exceedingly useful Bibliography.

Jenks, *Early History of Negotiable Instruments*, in *Law Quarterly Review*, vol. ix.

Lastig, *Entwickelungswege des Handelsrechts*, 1877.

Lattes, *Il Diritto Commerciale nella Legislazione Statuaria delle Città Italiane*, 1884.

Lattes, *Studii di Diritto Statuario*.

Morel, *Les Juridictions Commerciales au Moyen Age*, 1897.

Pertile, *Storia del Diritto Italiano*, 1896—1903.

Pollock and Maitland, *History of English Law*, 1898.

Pollock, *Principles of Contract*, 1902.

Rezzara, *Dei Mediatori e del Contratto di Mediazione*, 1903.

Scrutton, *Elements of Commercial Law*, 1891.

Silberschmidt, *Die Entstehung des Deutschen Handelsgerichts*, 1894.

Smith, *Mercantile Law*, 1890.

Sohm, *Die Entstehung des deutschen Städtewesens*, 1900.

Stevens, *Commercial Law*, 1903.

Thaller, *Traité Élémentaire de Droit Commercial*, 1900.

Thaller, *Les Sociétés par Actions dans l'Ancienne France*.

Viollet, *Histoire du Droit Civil Français*, 1893.

Wagner, *Seerecht*, 1884.

INDEX.

Abelard, Gervase, admiral of the fleet of the Cinque ports, 74

Acton Burnell, statute of (1283), 116

Admiralty courts, 15, 20, 40, 48, 61, 74 ff., 159

Agency, law of, 83

Agreements, inviolability of, 103

Amalfi, code of, 5, 49 f.

Ansaldus, 17th century jurist, 135 f.

Apprentices and masters, legal relations of, 84 f.

Aquila, consuls of (1396), 16

Aragonese kingdom, sea consulate of, 56 f., 61, 64

Aubaine, the right of, 86 ff.

Baldo, 14th century jurist, 104, 129

Barcelona, consulate of, 45, 56, 62 f.; laws of, 5, 21, 153 f., 159

Bartolo, 14th century jurist, 104

Beaumanoir, 98, 103

Bergamo, gild statutes of (1457), 16

Bills of exchange, 21, 34 ff., 82, 130

Blancard, M., edition of commercial documents of Marseilles, 107

Bologna, consuls of (1279), 17

Bonds of record, 115

Bosco, 15th century jurist, 149, 151

Bowen, Lord, on the practice of merchants, 102

Bracton, on stolen goods, 96

Bremen, charter of (965), 26

Brescia, statutes of (1313, 1429), 41, 44

Bristol treatise (14th century) on the Lex Mercatoria, 7, 11, 13 f., 20, 73, 84

Britton, on stolen goods, 95

Brokers, official position of, 90 ff.

Buller, Judge, on the Lex Mercatoria, 16

Calimala gild of Florence, statutes of (1301), 53, 122, 131, 134, 143

Canon law, 13, 103 f., 158 f.

Capitaneus, 53

Captain of the Lombards, 53, 87

Carlovingian rulers, 22 f., 119

Carta Mercatoria of Edward I., 3, 6

Chalon-sur-Saône, fair of, 88

Champagne, great fairs of, 2, 6, 37, 52 f., 67 f., 73, 87, 111 f., 135

Chapelande, fair charter of (1075), 98

Charlemagne, letter to Offa, 23

Chios, conquest of, 138

Collectors, later name for sea consuls, 49

Collegantia, the partnership so called, 126

Colonial enterprise, growth of, 137 ff.

Commenda, common form of partnership, 124 ff., 136 f.

Commendator, 127 ff.

Commercial courts, 39 ff., 67 ff.

Commercial statutes of Italy, 30 ff.

Common law courts, 76 ff.

Como, statutes of (1281), 41
Compagnia, partnership so
 called, 129
Compagnie des Iles d'Amérique,
 139
Conservator of a fair, office of, 68
Consideration, English doctrine
 of, 107
Consulad del Mare of Barcelona,
 45
Consular judges of Paris, 67
Consules electi, 51 f.
Consules hospites, 51, 54
Consules maris of Pisa, 48
Consules mercatorum, 32, 41
Consules missi, 51 ff.
Consuls, jurisdiction of, 40 ff.
Creditor, safeguarding interests
 of, 108, 120 f.
Cremona, statutes of (1388), 91
Curia legis of Pisa, 45 f.
Curia maris of Pisa, 45
Curia mercati, 73
Curia usus of Pisa, 45 f., 56
Custodes nundinarum, 67
Custom in Law Merchant, 10 f.

Davies, Sir John, on the Law
 Merchant, 1
Debts, acknowledgements of,
 106 ff.; recovery of, 116 ff.
Del Beni, Florentine house of,
 143
Dissolution of partnerships, 131
Dutch East India Company, 139

Earnest money, 3 ff.
East India Company, 139 f.
Edward I., statutes of, 3, 6, 37,
 112, 116, 118, 121
Elizabeth, Queen of Hungary,
 charter of (1381), 122
Emendatores, 31
Equity in Law Merchant, 16 f.

Factors of merchants, 83
Fair bonds, 6, 110 f., 120, 159
Fairs and markets, jurisdiction
 over, 22 ff.
Fairs, courts held in, 5 ff., 30,
 39, 68, 72

Filii familias, legal position of,
 83
Fleta, 3
Florence, 122 f.; city statutes
 of (1415), 44
Foreign merchants, disabilities
 of, 85 ff.
Foreigners, judged by the Law
 Merchant, 5 f., 20
Formal contracts, 102
Formless contracts, 102 ff.
Frankfort, 70
Frederick II., 5, 24, 86
Freiburg, charter of (1120), 28

Genoa, 32 ; sea consuls of, 49 ;
 Rota of, 134; colonial com-
 pany of, 138 f.; laws of, re-
 garding insurance, 153 f.
Germanic law, 83, 93, 100, 102,
 119
Gild court, jurisdiction of the,
 41 ff.
Gild Merchant, 32
"Go to host," 89
God's penny, 3
Good faith, principle of, 102 ff.,
 108
Grands Jours of Troyes, 68

Hanse, the German, 15
Hanse-reeve, jurisdiction of,
 70 f.
Helsmarshauser charter (997),
 25
Henry V. of England, 123
Hildesheim, 5
Holt, Lord, 77, 161
Horace, 90
Hostiensis, 13th century canon-
 ist, 103

Insurance, statute on (1601),
 11 ; legal principle of, 21,
 141 ff.
Interest, 159
International law, 113 f., 123 f.

James I. of Aragon, 56
Jerusalem, Assize of, 103
Jews, 100

John, King, of Aragon, 65
Joint-stock companies, 137 ff.
Jus Albanagii, 86

Kohler, quoted, 130

Lattes, quoted, 160
Leicester charter of 1277, 18 ff.
Leipzig, commercial court established (1682), 71
Lettres de foires, 2
Livre des assises de la cour des bourgeois, 141 f.
Lombard merchants, 109
Lombard gilds, 36
Lombard towns, 29, 33
Louis XI., 65
Lubeck, laws of, 21
Lyons, fair court at, 68 f.

Majorca, sea consulate of, 62 f.
Malynes, 157
Mansfield, Lord, 77, 107, 161
Manuel, Emperor, 52
Marchands de l'eau, Paris court of, 66
Maritime courts, 40, 70, 72 ff.
Maritime law, 5, 15, 40
Market courts, 30, 39
Marquardus, 157
Married women, legal position of, 82
Marseilles, commercial judges of, 15, 17, 66; sea code of, 21; commercial documents of, 107 ff., 133
Master and servant, legal relations of, 84
Meppen, market charter of (946), 24 f.
Merchant gilds, 31 f., 41, 55, 79 f.
Merchant judge, 55, 69, 71
Merchants, Italian, union of, 53; special protection of, 25 ff.; town quarters of, 52
Merovingian Empire, 22
Messina, sea consuls of, 64
Montpelier, sea consuls of, 65

Narbonne, elective consuls of, 66

Neapolitan charter (1115), 24
Nice, statutes of, 98
Notarial contracts, 108
Notaries, public, continental system of, 108 ff.
Notker, 10 f., 26
Novel disseisin, writ of, 118
Nuda pacta, 103, 105, 107
Nuremberg, charter of (1508), 71

Offene Gesellschaft, 137
Oleron, laws of, 5, 21.
Ordo maris of Pisa, 45

Padstow, maritime court of, 73
Panormitain, Archbishop of Palermo, 103
Paris, court of commerce of, 82; Parliament of, 68, 73
Parloir aux bourgeois, 66
Partnership, contracts of, 124 ff.
Pegolotti's "Practica della Mercatura," 142
Penalties, power to inflict, 53
Perpignan, sea consulate of, 65
Peter. IV. of Aragon, 62
Philip Augustus, 66, 122
Phocaea, conquest of, 138
Phraseology, legal, uniformity of, 108
Piacenza, monastery of, 24; merchant gild regulations of, 30 f., 91; statutes of (c. 1200), 51; (1323), 105
Piratical proclivities, 48, 74
Pisa, laws of, 20; constitutum usus of, 30 f.; curia maris of, 45; several courts of, 45 f.; sea consuls of, 45, 49 f.; 12th century law of, 51; commercial connection with Aragon, 56 f.
Pope, Hugo, case of, 84, 167
Preston, custumal of, 3
Principal and agent, relation of, 84 f.
Procurations, special or general, regarding partners, 132 ff.
Proxenos, Greek official, 54

Prudhommes of the sea and of merchants, when to be consulted, 59 f.

Public loans, 138

Real contracts, 102
Regensburg, hanse-reeve of, 70 f.
Registration of partners, 131 f.
Representation, direct, in partnerships, 129 f.
Reprisal, right of, 122 f.
Richard II., statute of (1390), 75 f.
Rolandinus, 121
Roman law, 69 f., 77, 82 f., 93, 103 f., 108 f., 158 ff.
Roman Rota, 135

Sales in markets and fairs, 93 ff.
Sea consulate, 48 ff., 57, 65
Sea gild of Pisa, 45
Seneschal, duties of, 68
Societas, partnership so called, 126, 129, 136 f.
Société en commandite, 129, 137
Société en nom collectif, 137
Solidarity of partners, 135
St Denis, fair of, 22
St George, bank of, 138
St Ives, fair court of, 5, 17, 73, 84, 99, 105, 156
Stade fair, charter of (1038), 24
Staple, court of the, 72 ff.
Staple, Ordinance of the (1353), 113, 118, 121
Stolen property, 93 ff.
Straccha, 157
Sub-merchants and masters, relations of, 84 f.

Summary procedure in Law Merchant, 12 f.

Tartagnus, Alexander (15th century jurist), 133
Tiel, merchants of, 11, 26
Town custumals, 35 ff.
Town, Law of the, Law Merchant an integral part of, 28
Tractator, 127 f.
Trani, sea consuls and maritime code of, 49 f.
Troyes, Grands Jours of, 68
Tuscan gilds, 36
Tuscan towns, 29

Ulpian, on brokers, 90
Usury, 158 f.

Valencia, sea consulate and maritime law of, 49, 57 ff.
Varese, 4
Venice, decree of council of (1287), 17 ; dispute between gild and city authorities of, 44 f.
Verona, gild statute of (1318), 133
Vienna, decree of town council of (1348), 90
Viollet's history of French law, 120
Von Freyberg, 71

Westminster, statute of (1275), 6
Wisby, laws of, 5

Ypres, fair and law of, 2, 6, 109 f., 120, 122